Curr Lib
QA107 .I58 1998
gr. 2
Investigations in number,
data, and space [kit].

INVESTIGATIONS IN NUMBER, DATA, AND SPACE

Sorting and Classifying Data

Does It Walk, Crawl, or Swim?

Grade 2

Also appropriate for Grade 3

Susan Jo Russell

Rebecca B. Corwin

Karen Economopoulos

Developed at TERC, Cambridge, Massachusetts

Dale Seymour Publications®

White Plains, New York

MURDOCK LEARNING RESOURCE CENTER
GEORGE FOX UNIVERSITY
NEWBERG, OR. 97132

WITHDRAWN

Some material in this unit was developed by Susan Jo Russell and Rebecca B. Corwin for *Sorting: Groups and Graphs* (a unit in the series *Used Numbers: Real Data in the Classroom*), © 1990 by Dale Seymour Publications®.

The *Investigations* curriculum was developed at TERC (formerly Technical Education Research Centers) in collaboration with Kent State University and the State University of New York at Buffalo. The work was supported in part by National Science Foundation Grant No. ESI-9050210. TERC is a nonprofit company working to improve mathematics and science education. TERC is located at 2067 Massachusetts Avenue, Cambridge, MA 02140.

This project was supported, in part, by the
National Science Foundation
Opinions expressed are those of the authors and not necessarily those of the Foundation

Managing Editor: Catherine Anderson
Grade-Level Editor: Alison Abrohms
Series Editor: Beverly Cory
Revision Team: Laura Marshall Alavosus, Ellen Harding, Patty Green Holubar, Suzanne Knott, Beverly Hersh Lozoff
ESL Consultant: Nancy Sokol Green
Production/Manufacturing Director: Janet Yearian
Production/Manufacturing Coordinator: Amy Changar, Shannon Miller
Design Manager: Jeff Kelly
Design: Don Taka
Illustrations: Laurie Harden, Susan Jaekel, Meryl Treatner
Cover: Bay Graphics
Composition: Archetype Book Composition

This book is published by Dale Seymour Publications®, an imprint of Addison Wesley Longman, Inc.

Dale Seymour Publications
10 Bank Street
White Plains, NY 10602
Customer Service: 1-800-872-1100

Copyright © 1998 by Dale Seymour Publications®.
All rights reserved. Printed in the United States of America.

Limited reproduction permission: The publisher grants permission to individual teachers who have purchased this book to reproduce the blackline masters as needed for use with their own students. Reproduction for an entire school or school district or for commercial use is prohibited.

DALE SEYMOUR PUBLICATIONS®

Order number DS43802
ISBN 1-57232-655-7
5 6 7 8 9 10-ML-02 01 00

Printed on Recycled Paper

TERC

INVESTIGATIONS IN NUMBER, DATA, AND SPACE®

Principal Investigator   Susan Jo Russell

Co-Principal Investigator   Cornelia Tierney

Director of Research and Evaluation   Jan Mokros

Director of K–2 Curriculum   Karen Economopoulos

Curriculum Development
Joan Akers
Michael T. Battista
Mary Berle-Carman
Douglas H. Clements
Karen Economopoulos
Anne Goodrow
Marlene Kliman
Jerrie Moffett
Megan Murray
Ricardo Nemirovsky
Andee Rubin
Susan Jo Russell
Cornelia Tierney
Tracey Wright

Evaluation and Assessment
Mary Berle-Carman
Jan Mokros
Andee Rubin

Teacher Support
Anne Goodrow
Liana Laughlin
Jerrie Moffett
Megan Murray
Tracey Wright

Technology Development
Michael T. Battista
Douglas H. Clements
Julie Sarama

Video Production
David A. Smith
Judy Storeygard

Administration and Production
Irene Baker
Amy Catlin
Amy Taber

*Cooperating Classrooms
for This Unit*
Caroline Chin
Boston Public Schools

Sylvia Aquino
New York City Public Schools

Cathy Gruetter
*Clarke County Public Schools
Georgia*

Consultants and Advisors
Deborah Lowenberg Ball
Marilyn Burns
Ann Grady
James J. Kaput
Mary M. Lindquist
John Olive
Leslie P. Steffe
Grayson Wheatley

Graduate Assistants
Kathryn Battista
Caroline Borrow
Judy Norris
Kent State University

Julie Sarama
Sudha Swaminathan
Elaine Vukelic
State University of New York at Buffalo

Revisions and Home Materials
Cathy Miles Grant
Marlene Kliman
Margaret McGaffigan
Megan Murray
Kim O'Neil
Andee Rubin
Susan Jo Russell
Lisa Seyferth
Myriam Steinback
Judy Storeygard
Anna Suarez
Cornelia Tierney
Carol Walker
Tracey Wright

CONTENTS

WHERE TO START

The first-time user of *Does It Walk, Crawl, or Swim?* should read
the following:

When you next teach this same unit, you can begin to read more of the
background. Each time you present the unit, you will learn more about
how your students understand the mathematical ideas.

Investigations in Number, Data, and Space® is a K–5 mathematics curriculum with four major goals:

- to offer students meaningful mathematical problems
- to emphasize depth in mathematical thinking rather than superficial exposure to a series of fragmented topics
- to communicate mathematics content and pedagogy to teachers
- to substantially expand the pool of mathematically literate students

The *Investigations* curriculum embodies a new approach based on years of research about how children learn mathematics. Each grade level consists of a set of separate units, each offering 2–8 weeks of work. These units of study are presented through investigations that involve students in the exploration of major mathematical ideas.

Approaching the mathematics content through investigations helps students develop flexibility and confidence in approaching problems, fluency in using mathematical skills and tools to solve problems, and proficiency in evaluating their solutions. Students also build a repertoire of ways to communicate about their mathematical thinking, while their enjoyment and appreciation of mathematics grows.

The investigations are carefully designed to invite all students into mathematics—girls and boys, members of diverse cultural, ethnic, and language groups, and students with different strengths and interests. Problem contexts often call on students to share experiences from their family, culture, or community. The curriculum eliminates barriers—such as work in isolation from peers, or emphasis on speed and memorization—that exclude some students from participating successfully in mathematics. The following aspects of the curriculum ensure that all students are included in significant mathematics learning:

- Students spend time exploring problems in depth.
- They find more than one solution to many of the problems they work on.

- They invent their own strategies and approaches, rather than rely on memorized procedures.
- They choose from a variety of concrete materials and appropriate technology, including calculators, as a natural part of their everyday mathematical work.
- They express their mathematical thinking through drawing, writing, and talking.
- They work in a variety of groupings—as a whole class, individually, in pairs, and in small groups.
- They move around the classroom as they explore the mathematics in their environment and talk with their peers.

While reading and other language activities are typically given a great deal of time and emphasis in elementary classrooms, mathematics often does not get the time it needs. If students are to experience mathematics in depth, they must have enough time to become engaged in real mathematical problems. We believe that a minimum of 5 hours of mathematics classroom time a week—about an hour a day—is critical at the elementary level. The scope and pacing of the *Investigations* curriculum are based on that belief.

We explain more about the pedagogy and principles that underlie these investigations in Teacher Notes throughout the units. For correlations of the curriculum to the NCTM Standards and further help in using this research-based program for teaching mathematics, see the following books, available from Dale Seymour Publications:

- *Implementing the* Investigations in Number, Data, and Space® *Curriculum*
- *Beyond Arithmetic: Changing Mathematics in the Elementary Classroom* by Jan Mokros, Susan Jo Russell, and Karen Economopoulos

This book is one of the curriculum units for *Investigations in Number, Data, and Space.* In addition to providing part of a complete mathematics curriculum for your students, this unit offers information to support your own professional development. You, the teacher, are the person who will make this curriculum come alive in the classroom; the book for each unit is your main support system.

Although the curriculum does not include student textbooks, reproducible sheets for student work are provided in the unit and are also available as Student Activity Booklets. Students work actively with objects and experiences in their own environment and with a variety of manipulative materials and technology, rather than with a book of instruction and problems. We strongly recommend use of the overhead projector as a way to present problems, to focus group discussion, and to help students share ideas and strategies.

Ultimately, every teacher will use these investigations in ways that make sense for his or her particular style, the particular group of students, and the constraints and supports of a particular school environment. Each unit offers information and guidance for a wide variety of situations, drawn from our collaborations with many teachers and students over many years. Our goal in this book is to help you, a professional educator, implement this curriculum in a way that will give all your students access to mathematical power.

Investigation Format

The opening two pages of each investigation help you get ready for the work that follows.

What Happens This gives a synopsis of each session or block of sessions.

Mathematical Emphasis This lists the most important ideas and processes students will encounter in this investigation.

What to Plan Ahead of Time These lists alert you to materials to gather, sheets to duplicate, transparencies to make, and anything else you need to do before starting.

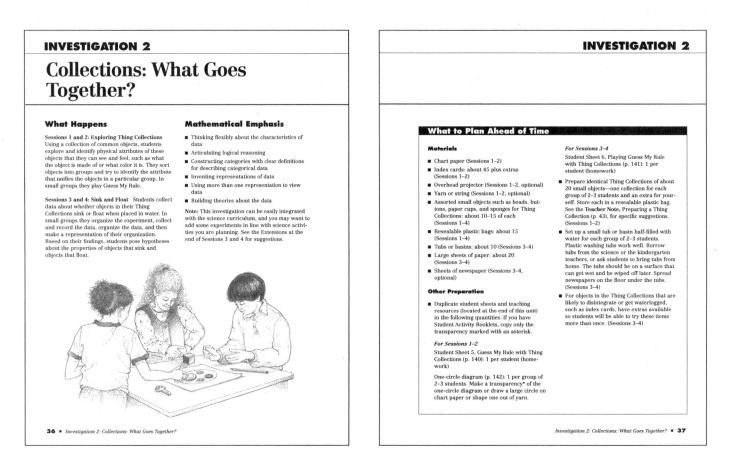

Sessions Within an investigation, the activities are organized by class session, a session being at least a one-hour math class. Sessions are numbered consecutively through an investigation. Often several sessions are grouped together, presenting a block of activities with a single major focus.

When you find a block of sessions presented together—for example, Sessions 1, 2, and 3—read through the entire block first to understand the overall flow and sequence of the activities. Make some preliminary decisions about how you will divide the activities into three sessions for your class, based on what you know about your students. You may need to modify your initial plans as you progress through the activities, and you may want to make notes in the margins of the pages as reminders for the next time you use the unit.

Be sure to read the Session Follow-Up section at the end of the session block to see what homework assignments and extensions are suggested as you make your initial plans.

While you may be used to a curriculum that tells you exactly what each class session should cover, we have found that the teacher is in a better position to make these decisions. Each unit is flexible and may be handled somewhat differently by every teacher. Although we provide guidance for how many sessions a particular group of activities is likely to need, we want you to be active in determining an appropriate pace and the best transition points for your class. It is not unusual for a teacher to spend more or less time than is proposed for the activities.

Classroom Routines The Start-Up at the beginning of each session offers suggestions for how to acknowledge and integrate homework from the previous session, and which Classroom Routine activities to include sometime during the school day. Routines provide students with regular practice in important mathematical skills such as solving number combinations, collecting and organizing data, understanding time, and seeing spatial relationships. Two routines, How Many Pockets? and Today's Number, are used regularly in the grade 2 *Investigations* units. A third routine, Time and Time Again, appears in the final unit, *Timelines and Rhythm Patterns*. This routine provides a variety of activities about understanding

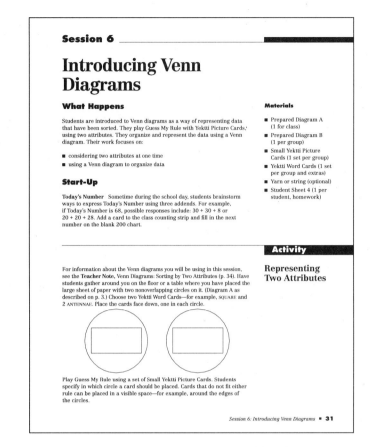

time; these can be easily integrated throughout the school day and into other parts of the classroom curriculum. A fourth routine, Quick Images, supports work in the unit *Shapes, Halves, and Symmetry*. After its introduction, you might do it once or twice a week to develop students' visual sense of number (as displayed in dot arrangements).

Most Classroom Routine activities are short and can be done whenever you have a spare 10 minutes—maybe before lunch or recess, or at the beginning or end of the day. Complete descriptions of the Classroom Routines can be found at the end of the units.

Activities The activities include pair and small-group work, individual tasks, and whole-class discussions. In any case, students are seated together, talking and sharing ideas during all work times. Students most often work cooperatively, although each student may record work individually.

Choice Time In most units, some sessions are structured with activity choices. In these cases, students may work simultaneously on different activities focused on the same mathematical ideas.

Students choose which activities they want to do, and they cycle through them.

You will need to decide how to set up and introduce these activities and how to let students make their choices. Some teachers set up choices as stations around the room, while others post the list of available choices and allow students to collect their own materials and choose their own work space. You may need to experiment with a few different structures before finding a set up that works best for you, your students, and your classroom.

Tips for the Linguistically Diverse Classroom At strategic points in each unit, you will find concrete suggestions for simple modifications of the teaching strategies to encourage the participation of all students. Many of these tips offer alternative ways to elicit critical thinking from students at varying levels of English proficiency, as well as from other students who find it difficult to verbalize their thinking.

The tips are supported by suggestions for specific vocabulary work to help ensure that all students can participate fully in the investigations. The Preview for the Linguistically Diverse Classroom lists important words that are assumed as part of the working vocabulary of the unit. Second-language learners will need to become familiar with these words in order to understand the problems and activities they will be doing. These terms can be incorporated into students' second-language work before or during the unit. Activities that can be used to present the words are found in the appendix, Vocabulary Support for Second-Language Learners. In addition, ideas for making connections to students' languages and cultures, included on the Preview page, help the class explore the unit's concepts from a multicultural perspective.

Session Follow-Up: Homework In *Investigations*, homework is an extension of classroom work. Sometimes it offers review and practice of work done in class, sometimes preparation for upcoming activities, and sometimes numerical practice that revisits work in earlier units. Homework plays a role both in supporting students' learning and in helping inform families about the ways in which students in this curriculum work with mathematical ideas.

Depending on your school's homework policies and your own judgment, you may want to assign more homework than is suggested in the units. For this purpose you might use the practice pages, included as blackline masters at the end of this unit, to give students additional work with numbers.

For some homework assignments, you will want to adapt the activity to meet the needs of a variety of students in your class: those with special needs, those ready for more challenge, and second-language learners. You might change the numbers in a problem, make the activity more or less complex, or go through a sample activity with those who need extra help. You can modify any student sheet for either homework or class use. In particular, making numbers in a problem smaller or larger can make the same basic activity appropriate for a wider range of students.

Another issue to consider is how to handle the homework that students bring back to class—how to recognize the work they have done at home without spending too much time on it. Some teachers hold a short group discussion of different approaches to the assignment; others ask students to share and discuss their work with a neighbor; still others post the homework around the room

and give students time to tour it briefly. If you want to keep track of homework students bring in, be sure it ends up in a designated place.

Session Follow-Up: Extensions Sometimes in Session Follow-Up, you will find suggested extension activities. These are opportunities for some or all students to explore a topic in greater depth or in a different context. They are not designed for "fast" students; mathematics is a multifaceted discipline, and different students will want to go further in different investigations. Look for and encourage the sparks of interest and enthusiasm you see in your students, and use the extensions to help them pursue these interests.

Excursions Some of the *Investigations* units include excursions—blocks of activities that could be omitted without harming the integrity of the unit. This is one way of dealing with the great depth and variety of elementary mathematics—much more than a class has time to explore in any one year. Excursions give you the flexibility to make different choices from year to year, doing the excursion in one unit this time, and next year trying another excursion.

Materials

A complete list of the materials needed for teaching this unit follows the unit overview. Some of these materials are available in kits for the *Investigations* curriculum. Individual items can also be purchased from school supply dealers.

Classroom Materials In an active mathematics classroom, certain basic materials should be available at all times: interlocking cubes, pencils, unlined paper, graph paper, calculators, and things to count with. Some activities in this curriculum require scissors and glue sticks or tape. Stick-on notes and large paper are also useful materials throughout.

So that students can independently get what they need at any time, they should know where these materials are kept, how they are stored, and how they are to be returned to the storage area. Many teachers have found that stopping 5 minutes before the end of each session so that students can finish their work and clean up is helpful in maintaining classroom materials. You'll find that establishing such routines at the beginning of the year is well worth the time and effort.

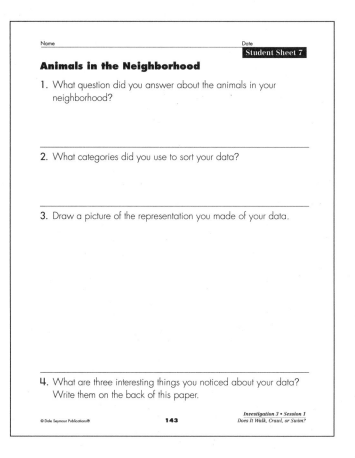

Student Sheets and Teaching Resources Student recording sheets and other teaching tools needed for both class and homework are provided as reproducible blackline masters at the end of each unit.

We think it's important that students find their own ways of organizing and recording their work. They need to learn how to explain their thinking with both drawings and written words, and how to organize their results so someone else can understand them. For this reason, we deliberately do not provide student sheets for every activity. Regardless of the form in which students do their work, we recommend that they keep their work in a mathematics folder, notebook, or journal so that it is always available to them for reference.

Student Activity Booklets These booklets contain all the sheets each student will need for individual work, freeing you from extensive copying (although you may need or want to copy the occasional teaching resource on transparency film or card stock, or make extra copies of a student sheet).

Computers and Calculators Calculators are introduced to students in the second unit of the grade 2 sequence, *Coins, Coupons, and Combinations*. It is assumed that calculators are readily available throughout the curriculum.

Computer activities are offered at all grade levels. Although the software is linked to activities in three units in grade 2, we recommend that students use it throughout the year. As students use the software over time, they continue to develop skills presented in the units. How you incorporate the computer activities into your curriculum depends on the number of computers you have available. Technology in the Curriculum discusses ways to incorporate the use of calculators and computers into classroom activities.

Children's Literature Each unit offers a list of related children's literature that can be used to support the mathematical ideas in the unit. Sometimes an activity is based on a selected children's book, with suggestions for substitutions where practical. While such activities can be adapted and taught without the book, the literature offers a rich introduction and should be used whenever possible.

Investigations at Home It is a good idea to make your policy on homework explicit to both students and their families when you begin teaching with *Investigations*. How frequently will you be assigning homework? When do you expect homework to be completed and brought back to school? What are your goals in assigning homework? How independent should families expect their children to be? What should the parent's or guardian's role be? The more explicit you can be about your expectations, the better the homework experience will be for everyone.

Investigations at Home (a booklet available separately for each unit, to send home with students) gives you a way to communicate with families about the work students are doing in class. This booklet includes a brief description of every session, a list of the mathematics content emphasized in each investigation, and a discussion of each homework assignment to help families more effectively support their children. Whether or not you are using the *Investigations* at Home booklets, we

expect you to make your own choices about homework assignments. Feel free to omit any and to add extra ones you think are appropriate.

Family Letter A letter that you can send home to students' families is included with the blackline masters for each unit. Families need to be informed about the mathematics work in your classroom; they should be encouraged to participate in and support their children's work. A reminder to send home the letter for each unit appears in one of the early investigations. These letters are also available separately in Spanish, Vietnamese, Cantonese, Hmong, and Cambodian.

Help for You, the Teacher

Because we believe strongly that a new curriculum must help teachers think in new ways about mathematics and about their students' mathematical thinking processes, we have included a great deal of material to help you learn more about both.

About the Mathematics in This Unit This introductory section summarizes the critical informa-

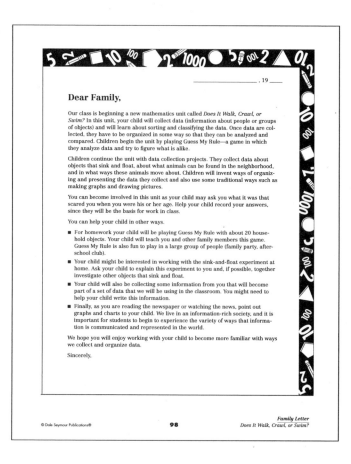

tion about the mathematics you will be teaching. It describes the unit's central mathematical ideas and the ways students will encounter them through the unit's activities.

About the Assessment in This Unit This introductory section highlights Teacher Checkpoints and assessment activities contained in the unit. It offers questions to stimulate your assessment as you observe the development of students' mathematical thinking and learning.

Teacher Notes These reference notes provide practical information about the mathematics you are teaching and about our experience with how students learn. Many of the notes were written in response to actual questions from teachers or to discuss important things we saw happening in the field-test classrooms. Some teachers like to read them all before starting the unit, then review them as they come up in particular investigations.

Dialogue Boxes Sample dialogues demonstrate how students typically express their mathematical ideas, what issues and confusions arise in their thinking, and how some teachers have guided class discussions.

These dialogues are based on the extensive classroom testing of this curriculum; many are word-for-word transcriptions of recorded class discussions. They are not always easy reading; sometimes it may take some effort to unravel what the students are trying to say. But this is the value of these dialogues; they offer good clues to how your students may develop and express their approaches and strategies, helping you prepare for your own class discussions.

Where to Start You may not have time to read everything the first time you use this unit. As a first-time user, you will likely focus on understanding the activities and working them out with your students. Read completely through all the activities before starting to present them. Also read those sections listed in the Contents under the heading Where to Start.

Preparing a Thing Collection — ⟨Teacher Note⟩

Collections of common objects give students the chance to explore similarities and differences in shape, color, texture, material, function, and a variety of other properties. Following are a few guidelines for putting together classroom Thing Collections.

- A collection of about 20 small objects provides enough variety and is a manageable size for second graders.

- As you choose objects, look for a few clear properties that are shared by four to eight objects. For example, you might include seven round things, five red things, six metal things, and four plastic things. Some objects might have more than one of these characteristics.

- Try to avoid too much variety in color so students will focus on other properties.

- You will need some objects that will sink and some that will float in water. Also include a few things that float for a while, then sink once they become waterlogged (index card), or things that sometimes sink and sometimes float, depending on how you put them into the water (paper cup).

- Because you will be playing Guess My Rule with the whole class, and each small group will be using its own collection, all the collections should be identical. For instance, if you include pipe cleaners, put the same colors in each collection. If you include paper clips, use the same size for everyone.

- Store each collection in a resealable plastic bag. (Sometimes students count the container as part of the collection, too.)

- You may want to exclude things that roll easily (like marbles) because they are hard to sort on flat surfaces.

- Keep a supply of duplicate objects, as some will inevitably be lost or broken, or will disintegrate when put in water.

You will probably have your own ideas for suitable objects that are readily available. A list of suggested items is given here.

index card
pipe cleaner
button
small paper clip
large paper clip
red checker
black checker
birthday candle
piece of sponge
plastic coffee can lid
drinking straw
rubber band
piece of string
peanut (in the shell)
sugar cube
piece of dry pasta
plastic drink stirrer
interlocking cube
craft stick (or tongue depressor)
piece of aluminum foil
jack
key
screw
toothpick
wooden bead
paper cup
penny
paint brush
pencil
tile
marker top

▮D▮I▮A▮L▮O▮G▮U▮E▮ ▮B▮O▮X▮

Paying Attention to the Evidence

During the activity, Guess My Rule: Thing Collections (p. 40) students try to figure out the teacher's mystery rule (THINGS THAT HAVE A POINT). Students have already guessed that a pencil, a jack, a paper clip, a screw and a plastic stirrer do fit the rule and that all other objects in the collection do not fit.

Graham [*waving his hand wildly*]: I know! I know!

What do you think, Graham?

Graham: It's THINGS THAT ARE METAL.

Why do you think that?

Graham: What?

How can you make us believe that the rule is THINGS THAT ARE METAL?

Graham: Well, the jack and the paper clip—

Helena: It can't be THINGS THAT ARE METAL because—

Wait, Helena, because I want to hear Graham's thinking about this. How were you thinking about it?

Graham: Well, I was thinking the screw and the paper clip were metal . . . [*stops, looks uncomfortable*]

Uh-huh. And do you want to think more about your idea?

Graham: Well, the pencil isn't metal, so I guess it can't be METAL THINGS.

Good thinking. Does anyone else see something to make you think THINGS THAT ARE METAL can't be the rule?

Helena: And the plastic stick isn't metal.

OK. My rule wasn't METAL. Any more ideas? This is a hard one. Tell me even if you had a good idea that you decided wasn't the rule. Did anyone have an idea you decided didn't work?

Phoebe: Well, I was thinking LONG THINGS until someone guessed the jack, and that's not long.

So you really used that clue. If I take the jack away, can anyone see a good reason why LONG THINGS still isn't the rule?

Bjorn: Yes, the craft stick isn't in the circle, and that's long.

OK, so Bjorn thought about the things that don't fit my rule. Remember, that's important to do. Who else is thinking about a rule that might work?

Olga: It's like, DIFFERENT SHAPES.

Tell us how you're thinking that DIFFERENT SHAPES works.

Olga: Well, like, the paper clip is like that [*shows the shape in the air*] and the jack is like a star.

And what did you think about the screw?

Olga: It's long.

And did they all go together somehow?

Olga: Yes, they're like, SHAPES.

Linda?

Linda: Well, it can't be SHAPES because the bead and the checker and the craft stick are all shapes and they don't fit.

Linda thinks that DIFFERENT SHAPES doesn't work because there are some shapes that don't fit my rule. Any other ideas?

Ebony: Not exactly long, but kind of long and pointy.

How would LONG AND POINTY THINGS work as the rule for the objects in the circle?

Continued on next page

The *Investigations* curriculum incorporates the use of two forms of technology in the classroom: calculators and computers. Calculators are assumed to be standard classroom materials, available for student use in any unit. Computers are explicitly linked to one or more units at each grade level; they are used with the unit on 2-D geometry at each grade, as well as with some of the units on measuring, data, and changes.

Using Calculators

In this curriculum, calculators are considered tools for doing mathematics, similar to pattern blocks or interlocking cubes. Just as with other tools, students must learn both *how* to use calculators correctly and *when* they are appropriate to use. This knowledge is crucial for daily life, as calculators are now a standard way of handling numerical operations, both at work and at home.

Using a calculator correctly is not a simple task; it depends on a good knowledge of the four operations and of the number system, so that students can select suitable calculations and also determine what a reasonable result would be. These skills are the basis of any work with numbers, whether or not a calculator is involved.

Unfortunately, calculators are often seen as tools to check computations with, as if other methods are somehow more fallible. Students need to understand that any computational method can be used to check any other; it's just as easy to make a mistake on the calculator as it is to make a mistake on paper or with mental arithmetic. Throughout this curriculum, we encourage students to solve computation problems in more than one way in order to double-check their accuracy. We present mental arithmetic, paper-and-pencil computation, and calculators as three possible approaches.

In this curriculum we also recognize that, despite their importance, calculators are not always appropriate in mathematics instruction. Like any tools, calculators are useful for some tasks but not for others. You will need to make decisions about when to allow students access to calculators and when to ask that they solve problems without them so that they can concentrate on other tools and skills. At times when calculators are or are not appropriate for a particular activity, we make specific recommendations. Help your students develop their own sense of which problems they can tackle with their own reasoning and which ones might be better solved with a combination of their own reasoning and the calculator.

Managing calculators in your classroom so that they are a tool, and not a distraction, requires some planning. When calculators are first introduced, students often want to use them for everything, even problems that can be solved quite simply by other methods. However, once the novelty wears off, students are just as interested in developing their own strategies, especially when these strategies are emphasized and valued in the classroom. Over time, students will come to recognize the ease and value of solving problems mentally, with paper and pencil, or with manipulatives, while also understanding the power of the calculator to facilitate work with larger numbers.

Experience shows that if calculators are available only occasionally, students become excited and distracted when they are permitted to use them. They focus on the tool rather than on the mathematics. In order to learn when calculators are appropriate and when they are not, students must have easy access to them and use them routinely in their work.

If you have a calculator for each student, and if you think your students can accept the responsibility, you might allow them to keep their calculators with the rest of their individual materials, at least for the first few weeks of school. Alternatively, you might store them in boxes on a shelf, number each calculator, and assign a corresponding number to each student. This system can give students a sense of ownership while also helping you keep track of the calculators.

Using Computers

Students can use computers to approach and visualize mathematical situations in new ways. The computer allows students to construct and manipulate geometric shapes, see objects move according to rules they specify, and turn, flip, and repeat a pattern.

This curriculum calls for computers in units where they are a particularly effective tool for learning mathematics content. One unit on 2-D geometry at each of the grades 3–5 includes a core of activities that rely on access to computers, either in the classroom or in a lab. Other units on geometry, measuring, data, and changes include computer activities, but can be taught without them. In these units, however, students' experience is greatly enhanced by computer use.

The following list outlines the recommended use of computers in this curriculum:

Kindergarten
Unit: *Making Shapes and Building Blocks*
   (Exploring Geometry)
Software: *Shapes*
Source: provided with the unit

Grade 1
Unit: *Survey Questions and Secret Rules*
   (Collecting and Sorting Data)
Software: *Tabletop, Jr.*
Source: Broderbund

Unit: *Quilt Squares and Block Towns*
   (2-D and 3-D Geometry)
Software: *Shapes*
Source: provided with the unit

Grade 2
Unit: *Mathematical Thinking at Grade 2*
   (Introduction)
Software: *Shapes*
Source: provided with the unit

Unit: *Shapes, Halves, and Symmetry*
   (Geometry and Fractions)
Software: *Shapes*
Source: provided with the unit

Unit: *How Long? How Far?* (Measuring)
Software: *Geo-Logo*
Source: provided with the unit

Grade 3
Unit: *Flips, Turns, and Area* (2-D Geometry)
Software: *Tumbling Tetrominoes*
Source: provided with the unit

Unit: *Turtle Paths* (2-D Geometry)
Software: *Geo-Logo*
Source: provided with the unit

Grade 4
Unit: *Sunken Ships and Grid Patterns*
   (2-D Geometry)
Software: *Geo-Logo*
Source: provided with the unit

Grade 5
Unit: *Picturing Polygons* (2-D Geometry)
Software: *Geo-Logo*
Source: provided with the unit

Unit: *Patterns of Change* (Tables and Graphs)
Software: *Trips*
Source: provided with the unit

Unit: *Data: Kids, Cats, and Ads* (Statistics)
Software: *Tabletop, Sr.*
Source: Broderbund

The software provided with the *Investigations* units uses the power of the computer to help students explore mathematical ideas and relationships that cannot be explored in the same way with physical materials. With the *Shapes* (grades 1–2) and *Tumbling Tetrominoes* (grade 3) software, students explore symmetry, pattern, rotation and reflection, area, and characteristics of 2-D shapes. With the *Geo-Logo* software (grades 2–5), students investigate rotations and reflections, coordinate geometry, the properties of 2-D shapes, and angles. The *Trips* software (grade 5) is a mathematical exploration of motion in which students run experiments and interpret data presented in graphs and tables.

We suggest that students work in pairs on the computer; this not only maximizes computer resources but also encourages students to consult, monitor, and teach each other. Generally, more than two students at one computer find it difficult to share. Managing access to computers is an issue for every classroom. The curriculum gives you explicit support for setting up a system. The units are structured on the assumption that you have enough computers for half your students to work on the machines in pairs at one time. If you do not have access to that many computers, suggestions are made for structuring class time to use the unit with fewer than five.

Assessment plays a critical role in teaching and learning, and it is an integral part of the *Investigations* curriculum. For a teacher using these units, assessment is an ongoing process. You observe students' discussions and explanations of their strategies on a daily basis and examine their work as it evolves. While students are busy recording and representing their work, working on projects, sharing with partners, and playing mathematical games, you have many opportunities to observe their mathematical thinking. What you learn through observation guides your decisions about how to proceed. In any of the units, you will repeatedly consider questions like these:

■ Do students come up with their own strategies for solving problems, or do they expect others to tell them what to do? What do their strategies reveal about their mathematical understanding?

■ Do students understand that there are different strategies for solving problems? Do they articulate their strategies and try to understand other students' strategies?

■ How effectively do students use materials as tools to help with their mathematical work?

■ Do students have effective ideas for keeping track of and recording their work? Do keeping track of and recording their work seem difficult for them?

You will need to develop a comfortable and efficient system for recording and keeping track of your observations. Some teachers keep a clipboard handy and jot notes on a class list or on adhesive labels that are later transferred to student files. Others keep loose-leaf notebooks with a page for each student and make weekly notes about what they have observed in class.

Assessment Tools in the Unit

With the activities in each unit, you will find questions to guide your thinking while observing the students at work. You will also find two built-in assessment tools: Teacher Checkpoints and embedded Assessment activities.

Teacher Checkpoints The designated Teacher Checkpoints in each unit offer a time to "check in" with individual students, watch them at work, and ask questions that illuminate how they are thinking.

At first it may be hard to know what to look for, hard to know what kinds of questions to ask. Students may be reluctant to talk; they may not be accustomed to having the teacher ask them about their work, or they may not know how to explain their thinking. Two important ingredients of this process are asking students open-ended questions about their work and showing genuine interest in how they are approaching the task. When students see that you are interested in their thinking and are counting on them to come up with their own ways of solving problems, they may surprise you with the depth of their understanding.

Teacher Checkpoints also give you the chance to pause in the teaching sequence and reflect on how your class is doing overall. Think about whether you need to adjust your pacing: Are most students fluent with strategies for solving a particular kind of problem? Are they just starting to formulate good strategies? Or are they still struggling with how to start? Depending on what you see as the students work, you may want to spend more time on similar problems, change some of the problems to use smaller numbers, move quickly to more challenging material, modify subsequent activities for some students, work on particular ideas with a small group, or pair students who have good strategies with those who are having more difficulty.

Embedded Assessment Activities Assessment activities embedded in each unit will help you examine specific pieces of student work, figure out what they mean, and provide feedback. From the students' point of view, these assessment activities are no different from any others. Each is a learning experience in and of itself, as well as an opportunity for you to gather evidence about students' mathematical understanding.

The embedded assessment activities sometimes involve writing and reflecting; at other times, a discussion or brief interaction between student and teacher; and in still other instances, the creation and explanation of a product. In most cases, the assessments require that students *show* what they did, *write* or *talk* about it, or do both. Having to explain how they worked through a problem helps students be more focused and clear in their mathematical thinking. It also helps them realize that doing mathematics is a process that may involve tentative starts, revising one's approach, taking different paths, and working through ideas.

Teachers often find the hardest part of assessment to be interpreting their students' work. We provide guidelines to help with that interpretation. If you have used a process approach to teaching writing, the assessment in *Investigations* will seem familiar. For many of the assessment activities, a Teacher Note provides examples of student work and a commentary on what it indicates about student thinking.

Documentation of Student Growth

To form an overall picture of mathematical progress, it is important to document each student's work. Many teachers have students keep their work in folders, notebooks, or journals, and some like to have students summarize their learning in journals at the end of each unit. It's important to document students' progress, and we recommend that you keep a portfolio of selected work for each student, unit by unit, for the entire year. The final activity in each *Investigations* unit, called Choosing Student Work to Save, helps you and the students select representative samples for a record of their work.

This kind of regular documentation helps you synthesize information about each student as a mathematical learner. From different pieces of evidence, you can put together the big picture. This synthesis will be invaluable in thinking about where to go next with a particular child, deciding where more work is needed, or explaining to parents (or other teachers) how a child is doing.

If you use portfolios, you need to collect a good balance of work, yet avoid being swamped with an overwhelming amount of paper. Following are some tips for effective portfolios:

- Collect a representative sample of work, including some pieces that students themselves select for inclusion in the portfolio. There should be just a few pieces for each unit, showing different kinds of work—some assignments that involve writing as well as some that do not.

- If students do not date their work, do so yourself so that you can reconstruct the order in which pieces were done.

- Include your reflections on the work. When you are looking back over the whole year, such comments are reminders of what seemed especially interesting about a particular piece; they can also be helpful to other teachers and to parents. Older students should be encouraged to write their own reflections about their work.

Assessment Overview

There are two places to turn for a preview of the assessment opportunities in each *Investigations* unit. The Assessment Resources column in the unit Overview Chart identifies the Teacher Checkpoints and Assessment activities embedded in each investigation, guidelines for observing the students that appear within classroom activities, and any Teacher Notes and Dialogue Boxes that explain what to look for and what types of student responses you might expect to see in your classroom. Additionally, the section About the Assessment in This Unit gives you a detailed list of questions for each investigation, keyed to the mathematical emphases, to help you observe student growth.

Depending on your situation, you may want to provide additional assessment opportunities. Most of the investigations lend themselves to more frequent assessment, simply by having students do more writing and recording while they are working.

Does It Walk, Crawl, or Swim?

Content of This Unit   This unit introduces students to sorting and classifying as a way of organizing data. Students investigate similarities and differences in sets of related objects, people, or data. They classify these groups according to particular attributes and sort the members of the group accordingly. Throughout the unit, data are collected in a variety of ways. In one activity, students design an experiment to collect data about objects that sink and float. Based on their organization of the data, they develop theories about why some things sink and some things float. While students are introduced to Venn diagrams and bar graphs as tools for organizing data, emphasis is placed on having students invent ways to organize and represent data so that they communicate information clearly, accurately, and in ways that make sense to them.

Connections with Other Units   If you are doing the full-year *Investigations* curriculum in the suggested sequence for grade 2, this is the third of eight units. The work in this unit is an extension of the data activities introduced in *Mathematical Thinking at Grade 2* and complements the work with numerical data that students will be doing in the seventh unit, *How Many Pockets? How Many Teeth?*

This unit can also be used successfully at grade 3, depending on the previous experience and needs of your students.

Investigations Curriculum ■ Suggested Grade 2 Sequence

Mathematical Thinking at Grade 2 (Introduction)

Coins, Coupons, and Combinations (The Number System)

▶ *Does It Walk, Crawl, or Swim?* (Sorting and Classifying Data)

Shapes, Halves, and Symmetry (Geometry and Fractions)

Putting Together and Taking Apart (Addition and Subtraction)

How Long? How Far? (Measuring)

How Many Pockets? How Many Teeth? (Collecting and Representing Data)

Timelines and Rhythm Patterns (Representing Time)

Investigation 1 ■ Sorting People and Yekttis

Class Sessions	Activities	Pacing
Sessions 1 and 2 (p. 4) COLLECTING AND REPRESENTING DATA ABOUT OURSELVES	Playing Guess My Rule Collecting and Recording Guess My Rule Data Representing Guess My Rule Data Representing Data with Categories Introducing Math Folders and Weekly Logs Homework: Guess My Rule Questions Extension: Playing Guess My Rule Extension: Integrating Addition and Subtraction	minimum 2 hr
Session 3 (p. 19) WORKING WITH TWO ATTRIBUTES	Guess My Rule: Two-Rule Version Generating Rules	minimum 1 hr
Sessions 4 and 5 (p. 23) LOOKING AT YEKTTIS	All About Yekttis Teacher Checkpoint: Guess My Rule 　with Yektti Cards Homework: Today's Number Extension: How Many in All? Extension: Using the Computer for Classification	minimum 2 hr
Session 6 (p. 31) INTRODUCING VENN DIAGRAMS	Representing Two Attributes Sorting by Two Rules Homework: Yektti Stories Extension: Guess My Rule with Words Extension: Other Attribute Materials	minimum 1 hr
Start-Up ■ Today's Number		

Mathematical Emphasis

- Examining carefully the differences and similarities in a group of related objects or related data

- Using negative information to clarify the definition of a category

- Sorting and classifying information

- Collecting, recording, and representing data

- Using more than one representation to view data

- Using Venn diagrams to show various relationships within a group of related objects

Assessment Resources

Observing the Students (p. 8)

Inventing Pictures of the Data
(Teacher Note, p. 16)

Keeping Track of Students' Work
(Teacher Note, p. 17)

Playing Guess My Rule (Dialogue Box,
p. 18)

Working with Two Rules (Dialogue
Box, p. 21)

Teacher Checkpoint: Guess My Rule
with Yektti Cards (p. 26)

Observing the Students (p. 27)

Describing the Set of Yekttis
(Dialogue Box, p. 30)

How Did You Know? (Dialogue Box,
p. 35)

Materials

Interlocking cubes

Overhead projector

Chart paper

Pencils, crayons, or markers

Index cards

Yarn or string

Math folders

Student Sheets 1–4

Family letter

Teaching resource sheets

Investigation 2 ▪ Collections: What Goes Together?

Class Sessions	Activities	Pacing
Sessions 1 and 2 (p. 38) EXPLORING THING COLLECTIONS	Exploring the Collections Guess My Rule: Thing Collections Describing the Collections Creating Sorting Rules Homework: Guess My Rule with Thing Collections Extension: Guess My Rule: Two Rules Extension: Making Classroom Collections	minimum 2 hr
Sessions 3 and 4 (p. 50) SINK AND FLOAT	What Sinks? What Floats? Teacher Checkpoint: Graphing Our Data Class Discussion: Why Things Sink and Float Publishing Our Results Homework: Playing Guess My Rule with Thing Collections Extension: More Science Experiments	minimum 2 hr

Start-Up ▪ Today's Number

Mathematical Emphasis

- Thinking flexibly about the characteristics of data

- Articulating logical reasoning

- Constructing categories with clear definitions for describing categorical data

- Inventing representations of data

- Using more than one representation to view data

- Building theories about the data

Assessment Resources

Paying Attention to the Evidence (Dialogue Box, p. 48)

Teacher Checkpoint: Graphing Our Data (p. 52)

Representing Sink-and-Float Data (Teacher Note, p. 54)

Second Graders' Theories About Sinking and Floating (Dialogue Box, p. 57)

Materials

Chart paper

Index cards

Overhead projector

Yarn or string

Assorted small objects

Resealable plastic bags

Tubs or basins

Large paper sheets

Newspaper

Student Sheets 5–6

Teaching resource sheets

Investigation 3 ▪ Animals in the Neighborhood

Class Sessions	Activities	Pacing
Session 1 (p. 60) HOW ANIMALS MOVE	Naming Animals That Live in Our Neighborhood Sorting Animals by How They Move Homework: Animals Near My Home	minimum 1 hr
Sessions 2 and 3 (p. 66) REPRESENTING DATA IN MORE THAN ONE WAY	Sharing Representations for How Animals Move How Else Can We Sort Animals? Making a Presentation Graph Extension: Collecting More Data	minimum 2 hr

Start-Up ▪ Today's Number, How Many Pockets?, Calculating the Total Number of Pockets

Mathematical Emphasis	Assessment Resources	Materials
▪ Constructing categories to describe data ▪ Articulating clear definitions of categories ▪ Organizing categorical data	Sorting Animals by How They Move: Observing the Students (p. 62) Animals in the Neighborhood (Teacher Note, p. 63) Does a Spider Walk? (Dialogue Box, p. 64)	Stick-on notes or index cards Chart paper Large paper sheets Crayons or markers Student Sheets 7–8

Investigation 4 ▪ Scary Things

Class Sessions	Activities	Pacing
Session 1 (p. 72) WHAT SCARES US?	Talking About Scary Things Our Most Scary Things Homework: Adult Scary Things Data	minimum 1 hr
Sessions 2 and 3 (p. 79) COMPARING SCARY THINGS DATA	What Scared Adults? Assessment: Organizing, Classifying, and Displaying the Data Comparing Scary Things of Adults and Students Choosing Student Work to Save Homework: Solving Problems with Imaginary Data Extension: Collecting More Data	minimum 2 hr

Start-Up ▪ **Today's Number**

Mathematical Emphasis

- Collecting and recording survey data

- Constructing categories to describe the data

- Comparing two data sets

- Experiencing the data analysis process

- Making presentation graphs and reporting on data analysis activities

Assessment Resources

What Are You Scared Of? (Dialogue Box, p. 77)

What Goes with Haunted Houses? (Dialogue Box, p. 78)

Assessment: Organizing, Classifying, and Displaying the Data (p. 80)

Choosing Student Work to Save (p. 82)

Assessment: Looking at Students' Data Representations (Teacher Note, p. 84)

Will the Same Categories Work? (Dialogue Box, p. 85)

Materials

Stick-on notes or index cards

Crayons or markers

Chart paper

Tape or thumbtacks

Half sheets of paper

Large paper sheets

There's a Nightmare in My Closet by Mercer Mayer (opt.)

Student Sheets 9–10

Following are the basic materials needed for the activities in this unit. Many of the items can be purchased from the publisher, either individually or in the Teacher Resource Package and the Student Materials Kit for grade 2. Detailed information is available on the *Investigations* order form. To obtain this form, call toll-free 1-800-872-1100 and ask for a Dale Seymour customer service representative.

Student math folders

Snap™ Cubes (interlocking cubes)

Assorted small objects for Thing Collections such as beads, buttons, paper cups, sponges. See the **Teacher Note**, Preparing a Thing Collection (p. 43).

Resealable plastic bags (about 15)

Tubs or basins (about 10)

Newspaper to spread under tubs or basins (optional)

Large sheets of paper, 18" by 24" (about 80 sheets)

Half-sheets of paper (about 100–150)

Index cards or stick-on notes (about 600)

Chart paper

Tape or thumbtacks

Pencils, crayons, or markers

Yarn or string (optional)

Overhead projector (optional)

Manufactured Yektti Cards (optional)

There's a Nightmare in My Closet, by Mercer Mayer (optional)

The following materials are provided at the end of this unit as blackline masters. A Student Activity Booklet containing all student sheets and teaching resources needed for individual work is available.

Family Letter (p. 98)

Student Sheets 1–10 (p. 99)

Teaching Resources:

Large Yektti Cards (p. 103)

Small Yektti Cards (p. 135)

Yektti Word Cards (p. 139)

One-Circle Diagram (p. 142)

Practice Pages (p. 147)

Related Children's Literature

Allen, Pamela. *Who Sank the Boat?* New York: Coward-McCann, 1982.

Baer, Edith. *This Is the Way We Go to School.* New York: Scholastic, 1990.

Carlson, Nancy. *Harriet's Halloween Candy.* Minneapolis: Carolrhoda Books, 1982.

Hoberman, Mary Ann. *A House Is a House for Me.* New York: The Viking Press, 1978.

Lobel, Arnold. "A Lost Button" from *Frog and Toad Are Friends.* New York: Harper & Row, 1970.

Mayer, Mercer. *There's a Nightmare in My Closet.* New York: Dial Books Young, 1990.

Reid, Margarette. *The Button Box.* New York: Dutton Children's Books, 1990

Selsam, Millicent E. *Benny's Animals.* New York: Harper & Row, 1966.

Slobodkina, Esphyr. *Caps for Sale.* Reading, Mass.: Addison-Wesley, 1968.

This unit focuses on collecting, organizing, and interpreting data that can be placed in categories. In primary grades, much of the data that interest children are categorical data—based on counting the members of certain related categories. For example, students might do a survey of the modes of transportation they use to get to school (how many walk, how many take the bus, how many ride a bicycle), or undertake a study of the weather throughout the year (how many days are cloudy, how many are sunny, how many are rainy). Students sort the data they collect into categories and make comparisons by counting.

This unit of study blends work in data analysis and work in classification. Classification involves complex thinking and is a critical tool in collecting, organizing, and interpreting data.

First, classification involves students in thinking flexibly about the characteristics of the data. Given a set of related things, such as neighborhood animals, we could focus on many different characteristics. Classification of animals is a real-world problem for scientists: What makes a bird a bird? Is a whale more closely related to a cow than to a trout? Which characteristics will reveal whether a raccoon is related to an opossum? Recent discoveries confirming that some birds are descended from dinosaurs show how startling the results of careful classification can be. In order to classify, students need to be flexible, paying attention to all the attributes of the thing they are studying. Students in the second and third grades are beginning to develop this flexibility, as their focus widens from single attributes to the relationships among more than one attribute. The attribute game Guess My Rule encourages this flexibility by leading students to observe different characteristics, sort collections in different ways, and describe similarities and differences in a group of things.

As students work with data they have collected, they make their own decisions about what categories to use and which data belong in which categories. Defining and redefining categories, as students do in the last half of the unit, is a critical part of data analysis. Sorting in various ways can reveal new aspects of the data. Each time we view the data somewhat differently we can gain new information about the world.

In data analysis, students use numbers to describe, compare, predict, and make decisions. When they analyze data, they search for patterns and attempt to understand what those patterns tell them about the phenomena the data represent.

A data analysis investigation generally includes recognizable phases:

- considering the problem
- collecting and recording data
- representing the data
- describing and interpreting the data
- developing hypotheses and theories based on the data

These phases often occur in a cycle: the development of a theory based on the data often leads to a new question, which may begin the data analysis cycle all over again.

Elementary students can collect, represent, and interpret real data. Although their work differs in many ways from that of adult statisticians, their processes are very similar. Elementary school students can both analyze data and use those data to describe and make decisions about real situations.

At the beginning of each investigation, the Mathematical Emphasis section tells you what is most important for students to learn about during that investigation. Many of these understandings and processes are difficult and complex. Students gradually learn more and more about each idea over many years of schooling. Individual students will begin and end the unit with different levels of knowledge and skill, but all will gain greater knowledge about how we collect, sort and classify, represent, describe, and interpret data.

Throughout the *Investigations* curriculum, there are many opportunities for ongoing daily assessment as you observe, listen to, and interact with students at work. In this unit, you will find two Teacher Checkpoints:

> Investigation 1, Sessions 4–5:
> Guess My Rule with Yektti Cards (p. 26)
>
> Investigation 2, Sessions 3–4
> Graphing Our Data (p. 52)

This unit also has one embedded assessment activity:

> Investigation 4, Sessions 2–3:
> Organizing, Classifying, and Displaying the Data (p. 80)

In addition, you can use almost any activity in this unit to assess your students' needs and strengths. Listed below are questions to help you focus your observations in each investigation. You may want to keep track of your observations for each student to help you plan your curriculum and monitor students' growth. Suggestions for documenting student growth can be found in the section About Assessment.

Investigation 1: Sorting People and Yekttis

- How do students think and talk about the similarities and differences in a group of related objects or data? Do they compare objects or data? Do they notice details?

- How do students use negative information to clarify the definition of a category? Do they look at data or objects *not* included in a group to help them determine what belongs in the group?

- How are students sorting and classifying information? Are they able to consider more than one attribute at a time? Can they ignore certain attributes to consider another? Can they group data by similar attributes? Can they place a previously placed item in a new category given a new classification scheme?

- How do students collect, record, and represent data? How are students organizing the information? Are they accurately representing the information? What materials and methods have they chosen to represent the data?

- Are students able to create more than one representation for a set of data? How do they view different representations of the same data? Do they understand that the same data can be represented in more than one way?

- How familiar are students with Venn diagrams? How do students place data or objects in a Venn diagram? Do they use evidence from objects already placed? the names of the categories? Do they place objects accurately? Can they describe the categories for each circle, the overlapping section, and the area surrounding the circles?

Investigation 2: Collections: What Goes Together?

- How flexible are students in their thinking about the characteristics of data? Are they able to consider more than one attribute at a time? Can they ignore certain attributes in order to sort by another? Can they group data by similar attributes? Can they create more than one classification system for a group of objects?

- How do students articulate their reasoning while classifying? How logical does their reasoning seem to be? What evidence do they use to support their reasoning?

- How do students describe categorical data? How do they create categories for the data? How clearly do they define those categories? Are they able to identify the attribute that unifies the objects in a particular group?

- What kinds of representations of data do students invent? How do they go about creating representations? How do they organize their work? Do their representations highlight important features of the data? Are they clear?

- Are students able to create more than one representation for a set of data? How do they view different representations of the same data? Do they understand that the same data can be represented in more than one way?

- Do students develop theories about the data? How? What kinds of hypotheses are students able to pose based on data? What kind of evidence do they use? Do their theories inspire further investigation?

Investigation 3: Animals in the Neighborhood

- How do students create categories for the data? Are they able to identify the attribute that unifies the objects in a particular group?

- How clearly do students define categories for the data? Is it possible for another person to place objects or data into their categories?

- How do students organize categorical data? How flexible are they about defining new categories and changing or modifying old categories?

Investigation 4: Scary Things

- How do students go about collecting and recording survey data from the whole group? How do they keep track of data? Do they make sure they have data from every person? How?

- How do students construct categories to describe data? What reasoning do they use to support their definitions of categories and their placement of data into categories?

- When comparing two sets of data what kinds of similarities and differences do students notice? Do they develop theories to explain differences and similarities between the data sets?

- How do students engage in the data analysis process (collecting, organizing, representing, and interpreting data)? Which parts intrigue them the most? Do any of the phases of the process challenge them?

- What kinds of presentation graphs do students make to show the data? How do they go about making their graphs? Are they aware of the communicative function of their graphs? Are their graphs clear? How do students report on their data analysis activities?

In the *Investigations* curriculum, mathematical vocabulary is introduced naturally during the activities. We don't ask students to learn definitions of new terms; rather, they come to understand such words as *factor* or *area* or *symmetry* by hearing them used frequently in discussion as they investigate new concepts. This approach is compatible with current theories of second-language acquisition, which emphasize the use of new vocabulary in meaningful contexts while students are actively involved with objects, pictures, and physical movement.

Listed below are some key words used in this unit that will not be new to most English speakers at this age level, but may be unfamiliar to students with limited English proficiency. You will want to spend additional time working on these words with your students who are learning English. If your students are working with a second-language teacher, you might enlist your colleague's aid in familiarizing students with these words before and during this unit. In the classroom, look for opportunities for students to hear and use these words. Activities you can use to present the words are given in the appendix, Vocabulary Support for Second-Language Learners (p. 95).

flies, walks, crawls, swims, hops Students collect data about ways in which animals in the neighborhood move, then categorize these data and make a representation such as a graph.

Multicultural Extensions for All Students

Whenever possible, encourage students to share words, objects, customs, or any aspects of daily life from their own cultures and backgrounds that are relevant to the activities in this unit. For example:

- When students finish developing their descriptions of the Yekttis in Investigation 1, encourage them to share descriptions of any cultural fantasy characters they are familiar with. They might describe Irish leprechauns, Arabic jinns, or Tibetan yeti.

- For Investigation 2, include multicultural objects such as chopsticks and foreign coins when you are preparing the Thing Collections of small objects. Provide opportunities for students to become acquainted with the objects and to share information about them.

Investigations

Sorting People and Yekttis

What Happens

Sessions 1 and 2: Collecting and Representing Data About Ourselves   Students observe, classify, count, and record data about themselves. They play a game called Guess My Rule as a way of collecting information, then display that information using graphs or pictures.

Session 3: Working with Two Attributes
Students consider two attributes at a time as they play a slightly new version of Guess My Rule. As a class, they generate possible mystery rules and discuss how to organize or represent groups of people who fit both mystery rules as they play the game.

Sessions 4 and 5: Looking at Yekttis   Students are introduced to Yektti Cards. Yekttis are a fictional group of creatures who are related by common sets of attributes. Students sort and classify the cards by looking for related attributes.

Session 6: Introducing Venn Diagrams   Students are introduced to Venn diagrams as a way of representing data that have been sorted. They play Guess My Rule with Yektti Picture Cards, using two attributes. They organize and represent the data using a Venn diagram.

Mathematical Emphasis

- Examining carefully the differences and similarities in a group of related objects or related data
- Using negative information to clarify the definition of a category
- Sorting and classifying information
- Collecting, recording, and representing data
- Using more than one representation to view data
- Using Venn diagrams to show various relationships within a group of related objects

What to Plan Ahead of Time

Materials

- Interlocking cubes: class set (Sessions 1–2)
- Overhead projector (Sessions 1–2, optional)
- Chart paper (Sessions 1–2, 6)
- Pencils, crayons, or markers (Sessions 1–3)
- Index cards: about 30 (Session 3)
- Yarn or string (Session 6, optional)

Other Preparation

- Duplicate student sheets and teaching resources (located at the end of this unit) in the following quantities. If you have Student Activity Booklets, copy only the items marked with an asterisk.

For Sessions 1–2
Family Letter* (p. 98): 1 per student. Remember to sign and date the letter before copying.

Student Sheet 1, Weekly Log (p. 99): 1 per student. At this time, you may wish to duplicate a supply to last for the entire unit and distribute the sheets as needed.

Student Sheet 2, Guess My Rule Questions (p. 100): 1 per student (homework)

For Sessions 4–5
Large Yektti Cards* (p. 103): 1 set for the class. Copy on heavy paper and laminate or mount of cardboard for durability.

Small Yektti Cards (p. 135): 1 set per group of 3–4 students. Cut out each card. Copy on heavy paper and laminate or mount the cards on cardboard for durability.

Yektti Word Cards (p. 139): 1 set for class* and 1 set per group of 3–4 students. Cut out

each card. Copy on heavy paper and laminate or mount the cards on cardboard.

Student Sheet 3, Today's Number (p. 101): 1 per student (homework)

For Session 6
Student Sheet 4, Yektti Stories (p. 102): 1 per student (homework)

- Prepare a math folder for each student if you have not done so for a previous unit. (Sessions 1–2)
- Read the **Teacher Note,** Playing Guess My Rule (p. 15), to get ready for the game. (Sessions 1–2)
- Read about Yektti Cards in the **Teacher Note,** About the Yekttis (p. 29). (Sessions 4–5)
- Read the **Teacher Note,** Venn Diagrams: Sorting by Two Attributes (p. 34), to become familiar with using Venn diagrams. (Session 6)
- Construct Diagrams A and B, below. Prepare one copy of Diagram A on chart paper for the class by drawing two nonoverlapping circles. Prepare 1 copy of Diagram B on large drawing paper for each group of 3–4 students by drawing two overlapping circles with a diameter of about 20 inches each and an overlap of about 10 inches. You can also use loops of yarn or string. (Session 6)

Diagram A   Diagram B

Collecting and Representing Data About Ourselves

Materials

- Chart paper
- Interlocking cubes
- Pencils, crayons, or markers
- Student Sheet 1 (1 per student)
- Family letter (1 per family)
- Student math folder (1 per student)
- Overhead projector (optional)
- Student Sheet 2 (1 per student, homework)
- Plain paper (1 sheet per student)

What Happens

Students observe, classify, count, and record data about themselves. They play a game called Guess My Rule as a way of collecting information, then display that information using graphs or pictures. Their work focuses on:

- collecting information about a group of people
- sorting and classifying information
- counting and comparing sets of data
- using pictures, tallies, and graphs to organize and display data

Start-Up

Today's Number   Today's Number is one of the routines that are built into the grade 2 *Investigations* curriculum. Routines provide students regular practice in important mathematical ideas such as number combinations, counting and estimating data, and concepts of time. For Today's Number, which is done daily (or most days), students write number sentences that equal the number of days they have been in school. The complete description of Today's Number (p. 86) offers some suggestions for establishing this routine and some variations.

If you are doing the full-year grade 2 *Investigations* curriculum, you will have already started a 200 chart and a counting strip during the unit *Mathematical Thinking at Grade 2*. Write the next number on the 200 chart and add the next number card to the counting strip. Together as a class brainstorm ways to express the number.

If you are teaching an *Investigations* unit for the first time, here are a few options for incorporating Today's Number as a routine:

- **Begin with 1**   Begin a counting line that does not correspond to the school day number. Each day add a number to the strip and use this number as Today's Number.
- **Use the Calendar Date**   If today is the sixteenth day of the month, use 16 as Today's Number.

Once Today's Number has been established, ask students to think about different ways to write the number. Post a piece of chart paper to record their suggestions. You might want to offer ideas to help students get started. If Today's Number is 45, you might suggest 40 + 5, 15 + 30, or 20 + 25.

Ask students to think about other ways to make Today's Number. List their suggestions on chart paper. Occasionally as students offer suggestions, ask the group if they agree with the statements. In this way, students have the opportunity to confirm an idea that they might have had or to respond to an incorrect suggestion.

As students grow more accustomed to this routine, they will begin to see patterns in the combinations, have favorite kinds of number sentences, or use more complicated types of expressions. Today's Number can be recorded daily on the Weekly Log. (See p. 12.)

Playing Guess My Rule

Note: If you are doing the full-year grade 2 *Investigations* curriculum, students will be familiar with the game Guess My Rule, which was introduced in *Mathematical Thinking at Grade 2*. Students may be familiar with both the game and making representations of the data, in which case you can begin with a quick game of Guess My Rule, then proceed to the third session of this investigation. If students are unfamiliar with the game, or if you think they need more experience with it, follow this session as written.

Introduce this investigation by telling students that as part of their work in mathematics this year they will sometimes collect information or data about themselves and their families or about groups of people in the school. See the **Teacher Note**, What Are Data, Anyway? (p. 14), for an explanation of what factual information constitutes data. Students will figure out ways to organize and describe the information to find out something about those groups of people. One of the ways they will be organizing information is by thinking about the ways things can be grouped together.

Scientists and mathematicians often think about how things are the same and how they are different. Sometimes you might group things together in one way and sometimes in another way, depending on what you are looking for and talking about.

For example, some people might think that all second graders belong together because they are in the second grade. But other people might think that some second graders and some first graders belong together because they all like baseball, all read the same kinds of books, or all walk to school.

Focusing on characteristics of students in your classroom, give other examples of how students might go together in different ways.

We are going to play a game called Guess My Rule using students in our class. You will have to pay attention to a lot of different things and figure out how certain groups of students belong together. Let's try the game. I am going to think of a mystery rule. Some students fit my rule and some don't. You will guess what my rule is.

For these class demonstrations choose straightforward, visually obvious rules such as WEARING A WATCH, WEARING STRIPES, or WEARING SHORT SLEEVES. Tell students that you are going to group them by a characteristic that they can see, such as something they are wearing, and not a characteristic that they can't see, such as whether they like ice cream or have a dog. For more information on classifying, see the **Teacher Note**, Playing Guess My Rule (p. 15).

Choose two or three students who fit your rule and have them stand in a designated area where the class can see them.

I have a mystery rule that tells something about people in this class. It's something you can see. Some people fit my rule and some people do not. Lila, Ping, and Rosie, please stand by the chalkboard where everyone can see you.

Who thinks he or she knows someone who should stand with Lila, Ping, and Rosie? Don't tell me what my rule is yet! Right now I just want you to tell me who else you think goes in the group with these people.

Students take turns saying who they think might fit the rule. Tell those named to stand either with the group that fits the rule or with the group that does not fit the rule. Stress the importance of all the clues—both those that fit the rule and those that do not. Prolong the clue gathering until many students have had a chance to contribute guesses and most students have joined one group or the other. See the **Dialogue Box**, Playing Guess My Rule (p. 18), for examples of how clues are gathered as the game progresses.

When enough evidence has been gathered and you sense that most students have an idea about the rule, ask volunteers to tell what they think the rule might be and why. Students may come up with categories that fit the evidence but are not the rule you have in mind. If this happens, acknowledge good thinking even though it did not lead to your rule.

❖ **Tip for the Linguistically Diverse Classroom**   Ask students to point to the item that they think dictates the rule. For example, a student points to the watch on everyone standing by the chalkboard.

Collecting and Recording Guess My Rule Data

Before students return to their seats, record the data about the number of students who did and did not fit the rule on chart paper so it can be easily saved. If some students are still in their seats, have them place themselves into the appropriate group and then have the class count the number of students in each group. For example:

WEARING A WATCH: 11

NOT WEARING A WATCH: 15

❖ **Tip for the Linguistically Diverse Classroom** Draw pictures next to each item when recording the data. For example, use a picture of a watch next to WEARING A WATCH, and a picture of a universal sign for "no" over a watch for NOT WEARING A WATCH.

Continue playing more rounds of Guess My Rule. In at least one round, use the rule WEARING SHIRTS WITH STRIPES. You will need this information in the next activity. Each time, record the data in a different way in order to model a variety of ways of keeping track of data. You can use, for example, pictures, tallies, numbers, or checkmarks. Students may have other suggestions for recording data. Encourage variety and innovation. Record the data on chart paper.

Wearing a watch	√ √ √ √ √ √ √ √ √ √
Not wearing a watch	√ √ √ √ √ √ √ √ √ √ √ √ √ √
Shoes with laces	mmmmmmmmmmmmmmmmmmmmm
Shoes without laces	mmmmm
Wearing shirts with stripes	ＨＨＨ ＨＨＨ ＨＨＨ I
Not wearing shirts with stripes	ＨＨＨ ＨＨＨ

Looking at the collected data, ask students to figure out how many are in each group. You might ask them to combine the totals for each rule or compare the numbers for each group.

How many more people are WEARING SHIRTS WITH STRIPES than NOT WEARING SHIRTS WITH STRIPES?

If there are 26 students in our class and 16 are WEARING STRIPES, how many are NOT WEARING STRIPES?

If no one notices, ask students why they think that the total number for each data set is 26 (or whatever the total number of students in your class is).

Note: We have suggested some possible rules that can be used for collecting data. Some rules may not be descriptive of your classroom. For instance, in some schools all students wear uniforms or students are not allowed to wear sneakers. It is important to choose rules that are descriptive of the students in your class.

Representing Guess My Rule Data

Working in pairs, students choose one of the data sets collected during Guess My Rule and find a way to represent the information. They use interlocking cubes, pictures, numbers, or graphs.

Mathematicians have different ways of showing the information they collect so they can see it clearly and share it with other people. Sometimes they make pictures or graphs, and sometimes they build models. They call these *representations* of the data.

With your partner, choose a set of data that we collected during Guess My Rule. Make your own representation of the data in a way that is different from how we recorded it on the chart. You can use cubes or draw a picture of the data. For example, if you pick WEARING A WATCH, draw something so that someone who wasn't here could figure out how many people wore watches and how many did not.

Before students begin working, have them generate ideas about how they might make a representation of the data. The word *representation* may be unfamiliar to students. Using words like *picture, graph, chart,* or *model* along with *representation* may be helpful. As a way of getting students started, give an example like watches and ask students how they might organize a picture or graph and what materials they might use. The **Teacher Note**, Inventing Pictures of the Data (p. 16), provides some examples of pictures and graphs that second graders have made.

Make available paper and a variety of materials that students can use to make their representations. If some students are having difficulty getting started, help them decide which materials to use and then have them think about the two pieces of information they need to represent.

Observing the Students As students are working, circulate around the room and observe the following:

■ How are students organizing the information?

- Are they accurately representing the information?
- What materials and methods have they chosen to represent the data?

Ask students to explain their representations to you.

- Can they interpret their representations?
- Can they extract the important information from their representations?

Asking students to explain their work allows you to learn more about how they are thinking and helps them to clarify their thinking. As students talk about their work, they correct themselves or clarify aspects that do not make sense. Encourage partners to ask each other questions about their work.

Sharing Representations   Have students briefly share their representations by asking groups that worked with the same set of data to bring their representations to the front of the room.

Comment on the variety of representations and materials used. If you have time, ask partners to say one thing about their representations. Find a place in the classroom to display students' representations so everyone can get a close look at them.

Representing Data with Categories

When students organized their Guess My Rule data they were dealing with two groups, one group of students who fit the rule and another that didn't. In some cases, the students in the latter category could not be described in any other way. For example, with the rule WEARING A WATCH, students either are or are not wearing a watch, and the group without watches can't be categorized further. In contrast, the students in the group NOT WEARING SHIRTS WITH STRIPES could further be described in other categories relating to shirts.

Introduce this idea to students in the following way:

We collected some data about the number of people in our class WEARING SHIRTS WITH STRIPES and the number of peoples NOT WEARING SHIRTS WITH STRIPES. This gives us information about the type of shirts worn by some students in our class. But there is a whole group of students for whom the only thing we know about them is that they are not wearing shirts with stripes. What are some other categories we could use to further describe their shirts?

List students' ideas on the board or overhead projector. Help them organize their list of categories into a simple bar graph. Ask students who fit each category to stand up. Draw a square, an X, or a stick figure as a way of entering the data on the graph.

When all the data from your class have been recorded, ask students what types of things they can now tell about shirts worn by the students in their classroom.

What information does this graph tell us?

What can you say about the number of students wearing shirts with stripes compared to the number of students wearing shirts with writing?

How does this representation differ from the representation some of you made before using the Guess My Rule data?

Would these data change if we collected the same information tomorrow? Why or why not?

❖ **Tip for the Linguistically Diverse Classroom** Restructure some of the discussion questions so that they can be answered in one-word responses. For example: How many people are wearing shirts with stripes? How many students are wearing shirts with writing? Are more or fewer people wearing shirts with stripes?

Ask students how they might use the interlocking cubes to build a model that would represent their shirt data. Have pairs of students represent the data using the cubes.

Students will continue to collect, record, and interpret data in the next two sessions of this unit and in other units in the *Investigations* curriculum. Consider integrating data collection and representation into other areas of your curriculum, such as science or social studies. Collecting data about themselves is a wonderful way to help students get to know one another at the beginning of the school year.

Introducing Math Folders and Weekly Logs

If you are using the full-year *Investigations* curriculum, students will be familiar with math folders and Weekly Logs. If this curriculum is new to students, tell them about one way they will keep track of the math work they do.

Mathematicians show how they think about and solve problems by talking about their work, drawing pictures, building models, and explaining their work in writing so that they can share their ideas with other people. Your math folder will be a place to collect the writing and drawing that you do in math class.

Distribute math folders to students and have them label the folders with their names.

Your math folder is a place to keep track of what you do each day in math class. Sometimes there will be more than one activity to choose from, and at other times, like today, everyone in the class will do the same thing. Each day you will record what you did on this Weekly Log.

Distribute Student Sheet 1, Weekly Log, and ask students to write their names at the top of the page. Point out that there are spaces for each day of the week and ask them to write today's date on the line after the appropriate day. If you are doing the activity Today's Number, students can write the number in the box beside the date.

Ask students for suggestions about what to call today's activities. Titles for choices and whole-class activities should be short, to encourage all students to record what they do each day. List their ideas on the board and let students choose one title to write in the space below the date.

❖ **Tip for the Linguistically Diverse Classroom** Encourage students who are not writing comfortably in English to use drawings to record in their Weekly Log. If students demonstrate some proficiency in writing, suggest that they record a few words with their drawings.

Weekly Logs can be stapled to the front of the folders (each new week on the top so students can view prior logs by lifting up the sheets).

During the unit (or throughout the year), you might use the math folders and Weekly Logs in a number of ways:

- to keep track of what kinds of activities students choose to do and how frequently they choose them
- to review with students, individually or as a group, the work they've accomplished

- to share student work with families, either by sending folders home periodically for students to share, or during student/family/teacher conferences

For more information on students' work, see the **Teacher Note,** Keeping Track of Students' Work (p. 17).

Sessions 1 and 2 Follow-Up

Guess My Rule Questions   Students use data similar to what was collected while Playing Guess My Rule in small groups to investigate addition and subtraction strategies. On Student Sheet 2, Guess My Rule Questions, students are given sample data from an imaginary class. They are given the total number of students as well as the number of students who are wearing shoes with laces. They will figure out how many students are not wearing shoes with laces and draw a representation of the information.

Send home the family letter or *Investigations* at Home booklet.

Playing Guess My Rule   Students usually enjoy playing Guess My Rule so much that you can continue to play the game throughout the unit. One or two rounds with students will fit in nicely at odd times—before lunch, at the end of the day, or whenever you have a free 10 minutes.

Integrating Addition and Subtraction   Encourage students to think about addition and subtraction while collecting or analyzing data. For example, pose questions such as: "If there are 26 students in our class, and 9 are wearing watches, how many students are not wearing watches? How could we figure this out? Can we do it without counting?"

Homework

Extensions

What Are Data, Anyway?

I'm 48 inches tall.

This bottle holds 2 liters of soda pop.

She is wearing sneakers.

These shoes weigh 150 grams.

Each of these statements contains descriptive information or *data* about some person or thing. *Data* is a plural noun; one datum is a single fact. Data are the facts, or the information, that differentiate and describe people, objects, or other entities (for example, countries). Data may be expressed as numbers (he is 48 inches tall; she has 4 people in her family) or attributes (his hair is curly).

Data are collected through surveys, observations, measuring, counting, and experiments. If we study rainfall, we might collect rain and measure the amount that falls each day. If we study hair color, we might observe and record the color of each person's hair.

Collecting data involves detailed judgments about how to count, measure, or describe. Should we record rainfall data for each day or for each rainstorm? Should we round off to the nearest inch? Should we count just one color for a person's hair? Should we record "yellow" or "dirty blond" or "gold"? Should "brown" be a single category, or should it be divided into several shades?

Once data are collected, recorded, counted, and analyzed, we can use them as the basis for making decisions. In one school, for example, a study of accidents on a particular piece of playground equipment showed that most of the accidents involved children who were in first, second, or third grade. Those who studied the data realized that the younger students' hands were too small to grasp the bars firmly enough. A decision to keep primary-grade children off this equipment was made because the data, or the facts, led to that conclusion.

When students collect data, they are collecting facts. When they interpret these data, they are developing theories or generalizations. The data provide the basis for their theories.

Playing Guess My Rule

Guess My Rule is a classification game in which players try to figure out the common characteristic, or attribute, of a set of objects. To play the game, the rule maker (who may be you, a student, or a small group) decides on a mystery rule for classifying a particular group of things. For example, rules for people might be WEARING STRIPES or WEARING GLASSES.

The rule maker starts the game by giving some examples of people who fit the rule, for example, by having two students who are wearing blue stand up. The guessers then try to find other individuals who fit the rule: "Does Angel fit your rule?"

With each guess, the individual named is added to one group or the other—*does fit* or *does not fit* the rule. Both groups must be clearly visible to the guessers so they can make use of all the evidence—what does and does not fit—as they try to figure out what the rule is.

You'll need to stress two guidelines during play:

- *"Wrong" guesses are clues and just as important as "right" guesses.* "No, Jess doesn't fit, but that's important evidence. Think about how Graham is different from Karina, Juanita, Ping, and Jeffrey." This is a wonderful way to help students learn that errors can be important sources of information.

- *When you think you know what the rule is, test your theory by giving another example, not by revealing the rule.* "Naomi, you look like you're sure you know what the rule is. We don't want to give it away yet, so let's test your theory. Tell me someone who you think fits the rule." Requiring students to add new evidence, rather than making a guess, serves two purposes. It allows students to test their theories without revealing their guess to other students, and it provides more information and more time to think for students who do not yet have a theory.

When students begin choosing rules they sometimes think of rules either too vague (WEARING DIFFERENT COLORS) or too hard to guess (HAS A THREAD HANGING FROM A SHIRT). Guide and support students in choosing rules that are not so obvious that everyone will see them immediately, but not so hard that no one will be able to figure them out.

Students should be clear about who would fit their rule *and* who would not fit; this eliminates rules like WEARING DIFFERENT COLORS, which everyone will probably fit. It's also important to pick a rule about something people can observe. One rule for classifying might be LIKES BASEBALL, but no one can guess this rule by just looking.

Guess My Rule can be dramatic. Keep the mystery and drama high with remarks such as, "That was an important clue," "This is very tricky," "I think Tory has a good idea now," and "I bet I know what Carla's theory is."

It is surprising how hard it can be to guess what seems to be an obvious rule, like WEARING GREEN. It is often difficult to predict which rules will be hard to guess. A rule you think will be tough could be guessed right away, while a rule that seemed obvious might be impossible to guess.

Give additional clues when students are truly stuck. For example, one teacher chose WEARING BUTTONS as the rule. All students had been placed in one of the two groups, but still no one could guess. So the teacher moved among the students, drawing attention to each in turn: "Look carefully at Lionel's front. Now I'm going to turn Rosie around to the back, like this—see what you can see. Look along Naomi's arms." Finally, students guessed the rule.

Classification is a process used in many disciplines, and you can easily adapt Guess My Rule to other subject areas. Animals, states, historical figures, geometric shapes, and types of food can all be classified in different ways.

Inventing Pictures of the Data

When students invent their own ways of representing data, they often come up with pictures or graphs that powerfully communicate the meaning of the data. While many commonly used representations, such as bar graphs and tallies, should gradually become familiar to students, encourage them to use their own inventiveness and creativity to develop pictures and graphs as well. In this way, students make the data their own.

In the ongoing history of visual representation of data, many unusual forms of graphs and diagrams have been developed. Some of the most striking graphs were devised by a statistician or scientist to represent a single, unusual data set in a new way. Even now, new standard forms are taking their place in the statistician's repertoire beside the more familiar bar graph or histogram.

So, while we do want students to use and interpret standard forms of graphs, we also want them to learn that, like other mathematicians and scientists, they can picture data in their own, individual ways. These pictures or diagrams or graphs are tools in the data analysis process.

Through constructing their own representations, students can become more familiar with the data, understand the data better, begin to develop theories about the data, and, if they are going to "publish" their findings, communicate what they know about the data to an audience.

Graphs can be made with pencil and paper, interlocking cubes, and stick-on notes. Cubes and stick-on notes offer flexibility since they can easily be rearranged. Encourage students to construct concrete and pictorial representations of their data using interlocking cubes, pictures, or even the actual objects.

Encourage students to invent and use different forms until they discover some that work well in organizing their data. Students in the second grade are capable of inventing simple—but effective—sketches and pictures of the data they collect. Shown on this page are ways second graders have represented their Guess My Rule Data. These examples do not follow a standard graph or table form, but show the data clearly and effectively.

14 peple have darc hair
12 peple do not

darc hair   not darc hair

9 are waring a watch and
17 are not waring watch

waring watch

not waring watch

Keeping Track of Students' Work

Throughout the *Investigations* curriculum there are numerous opportunities to observe students as they work. Teacher observations are an important part of ongoing assessment. While individual observations are snapshots of a student's experience with a single activity, when considered over time they can provide an informative and detailed picture of a student. These observations can be useful in documenting and assessing a student's growth. They offer important sources of information when preparing for family conferences or writing student reports.

Your observations of students will vary throughout the year. At times you may be interested in particular strategies that students are developing to solve problems. Or you may want to observe how students use or do not use materials to help them solve problems. At other times you may be interested in noting the strategy that a student uses when playing a game. Class discussions also provide many opportunities to take note of students' ideas and thinking.

Keeping observation notes on a class of 28 students can become overwhelming and time-consuming. You will probably find it necessary to develop some sort of system to record and keep track of your observations of students. A few ideas and suggestions are offered here, but you will want to find a system that works for you.

A class list of names is a convenient way of jotting down observations of students. Since the space is limited, it is not possible to write lengthy notes; however, when kept over time these short observations provide important information.

Stick-on address labels can be kept on clipboards around the room. Notes can be taken on individual students and then these labels can be peeled off and stuck into a file that you set up for each student.

Alternatively, jotting down brief notes at the end of each week may work well for you. Some teachers find that this is a useful way of reflecting on the class as a whole and on the curriculum and on individual students. Planning for the next weeks' activities often develops from these weekly reflections.

In addition to your own notes on students, all students keep a folder of work. This work and the daily entries on the Weekly Logs can document a student's experience. Together they can help you keep track of the students in your classroom, assess their growth over time, and communicate this information to others. At the end of each unit there is a list of suggestions of things you might choose to keep in students' folders.

Playing Guess My Rule

In this discussion which occurs during the activity Playing Guess My Rule (p. 5), the class is trying to guess their teacher's mystery rule, WEARING STRIPES.

Lila and Graham both fit the rule I'm thinking of. Let's have people who fit my rule stand here. [*Lila and Graham stand up in front of the chalkboard.*] **Who thinks he or she knows someone else who might fit this group? Don't guess the rule; just tell me another person you think might fit.**

Lionel: Do I fit?

Yes, you do fit my rule. [*Lionel joins Lila and Graham. It happens that all three children have black hair. This characteristic is visually striking when they all stand together.*]

Phoebe [*who has black hair*]: I think I fit.

No, you don't fit my secret rule, but I bet I know what you were thinking of. Stand over by my desk to start the "people who don't fit the rule group." Phoebe is an important clue.

Salim: I know what the rule is! It's—

Don't say the rule yet. If you think you know, tell me someone else who fits.

Salim: Um … [*Looks around but can't find anyone*]

What about you?

Salim: I don't think I fit.

OK. Go stand with Phoebe so people have more clues for who doesn't fit.

[*Later*]

Lila: Does Camilla fit? [*Camilla is wearing striped pants.*]

Yes, she does fit. That's another important clue.

Simon: I know! I know!

Others: Me, too! I know the rule!

OK, let's see if anyone else fits the rule. Then you can say what you think it is.

In this conversation, the teacher keeps the focus on looking carefully at all the evidence rather than on getting the right answer quickly. The teacher uses Phoebe's sensible guess to point out the value of negative information. Even though Phoebe doesn't fit the rule, she provides an important clue by narrowing down the possibilities. By prolonging the discussion and gathering more clues, the teacher gives more students time to think about and reach their own conclusions.

Working with Two Attributes

What Happens

Students consider two attributes at a time as they play a slightly new version of Guess My Rule. As a class, they generate possible mystery rules and discuss how to organize or represent groups of people who fit both mystery rules as they play the game. Their work focuses on:

- sorting information according to attributes
- considering more than one attribute at a time
- exploring how to represent data with shared attributes

Start-Up

Today's Number Suggest that students use combinations of 10 in their number sentences. For example, if the number they are working on is 64, and one number sentence is $10 + 10 + 10 + 10 + 10 + 10 + 4$, ask students if there is another way of making 64, such as $(6 + 4) + (6 + 4) + (6 + 4) + (6 + 4) + (6 + 4) + (6 + 4) + 4$. Add a card to the class counting strip and fill in another number on the blank 200 chart. For complete details on this routine, see p. 86.

Materials

- Index cards
  (2 per group)
- Crayons or markers

Activity

Play Guess My Rule with students as you did in Session 1. You might want to start with one round of the game using a single rule to remind students how the game works. For the second round, choose two rules that will fit some students (for example, WEARING GREEN and HAS GLASSES).

Now I have a bigger challenge. This time I have two mystery rules in mind. You'll be trying to figure out both of them. Students who fit Rule 1 will stand over by the chalkboard. Jeffrey and Ebony fit my first rule. And I have another rule. Rule 2 students will stand by the windows. Phoebe and Trini fit Rule 2. This time when you choose someone, you have to tell me which rule you think the person fits.

As the game progresses, remind students to observe each group carefully and look for what the students in that group have in common.

At some point in the game, students will notice that some people belong in

Guess My Rule: Two-Rule Version

both groups. When this occurs (either during the game or when the rules have been guessed), ask them what they want to do about people who fit both rules. See the **Dialogue Box,** Working with Two Rules (p. 21), for suggestions on how to handle overlapping groups. Usually, students suggest that these people go in the middle or stand against a third wall. (If students do not bring up the overlap problem themselves, draw their attention to the issue of people who belong in both groups.)

When everyone has been assigned to the appropriate group, ask students to try to articulate a description for each group, including the group remaining in their seats. Not all students will be able to give precise descriptions. Encourage them to give at least partial descriptions and ask others to complete the descriptions.

Activity

Generating Rules

Students enjoy contributing the rules for Guess My Rule and offering suggestions for where students who fit both rules should stand. Organize students into groups of three or four and distribute two index cards to each group.

We are going to play this game again, but this time you will be thinking of the mystery rules to use in the game. Talk with your group members and decide on two rules that you think would be good to use. Write each rule on an index card. Talk quietly so other groups will not hear, and be careful not to show your index cards.

When most groups have recorded their rules, you can collect all the cards, mix them up, and draw out two. Use these two mystery rules for the next round of the game.

Wearing long pants

Caries a backpak

Note: For some pairs of rules, you may have students who fit in the overlap group, but for other pairs (for example, red hair and black hair) there will be no students in both categories. If this latter situation occurs, discuss it

Working with Two Rules

In this discussion during the activity Guess My Rule: Two-Rule Version (p. 19), the class is trying to guess the two mystery rules their teacher is using to group students.

I'm thinking of one rule for students standing by the chalkboard [*for example,* WEARING GLASSES] **and a different rule for students standing by the windows** [WEARING GREEN]. **I'll start out with Jeffrey and Ebony by the chalkboard, and I'm going to put Phoebe and Trini by the windows. Any ideas about who else might fit?**

Ayaz: I think Chen goes by the chalkboard.

Yes, he does fit there.

Laura: Does Paul go by the windows?

No, he doesn't fit there.

Laura: How about by the chalkboard?

Yes, Paul fits the rule I have for the group by the chalkboard. Who thinks he or she might know where Simon goes?

Harris: I don't think he goes in either place.

You're right. So what should Simon do?

Harris: He should just stay in his seat.

OK, Harris is suggesting that Simon stay in his seat because he doesn't fit either rule. Does everyone agree?

Juanita: Well, he should stand up.

Why should he do that?

Juanita: Because then we'll remember that we already tried Simon and he didn't fit anywhere.

OK, so that's how we'll tell who doesn't fit.

[*Later in the game*]

I think you're ready to guess the rule for the people by the windows.

Linda: It's GREEN.

Yes, my rule was WEARING GREEN. OK, everyone who is wearing green move over to the windows.

[*Several students from the "chalkboard group" start moving over to the windows.*]

But you're in the chalkboard group!

[*They look confused. One of the students starts moving back.*]

But you're in the green group!

Several students talking at once: Wait a minute. I'm in both. Jess has green and he's in the chalkboard group. Yes, and Chen has a green shirt, and he's in the chalkboard group, too.

You're right. But Chen and Jess do fit my rule for the chalkboard group and they're wearing green. Let's see if we can get the rule for the chalkboard group and then we'll have to figure out what to do about students who fit both my rules. Does anyone think he or she knows who else goes in the chalkboard group?

[*Later*]

OK, you guessed that the chalkboard group all are wearing glasses. Now we have all these students who are wearing glasses over here, and all these students who are wearing green over there. But what can we do about the students who are wearing both glasses and green? They can't just keep running back and forth!

Ebony: Well, all the students who are wearing both could go to a different place.

Graham: They could stand over by the door.

Laura: They could go in the middle, like kind of touching both groups.

How would that work?

Continued on next page

continued

Eventually all the students have been assigned to the chalkboard group (WEARING GLASSES), the window group (WEARING GREEN), the middle group (WEARING GLASSES AND GREEN), or are standing up at their seats (NOT WEARING GLASSES OR GREEN).

Now, who can tell me why some of you moved to the middle?

Rosie: Some kids wearing green also are wearing glasses.

Tim: If you have both things, you stand in the middle. If you have one thing, you stand at the side.

Who can pick one of the groups and say exactly what the rule is for that group? And don't forget the group that is standing near their seats. They're an important group, too!

Juanita: Well, the chalkboard group is wearing glasses.

It's true, I see glasses on everyone in the chalkboard group. But that's not the only place I see glasses. Can anyone add to Juanita's description?

Simon: The middle group has glasses, too.

Hmm, so how do I tell the difference?

Juanita: The middle group is wearing green and they're wearing glasses.

Trini: And the chalkboard group is wearing glasses and isn't wearing green!

What a clear way of putting it, Juanita and Trini. Can anyone else describe one of the groups? How about the group standing near their seats? That's a real challenge.

Looking at Yekttis

What Happens

Students are introduced to Yektti Cards. Yekttis are a fictional group of creatures who are related by common sets of attributes. Students sort and classify the cards by looking for related attributes. Their work focuses on:

- identifying attributes of a data set
- grouping data by similar attributes

Start-Up

Today's Number Suggest that students use doubles in their number sentences. For example, if the number they are working on is 66, possible combinations include: 33 + 33 or 11 + 11 + 11 + 11 + 11 + 11. Add the next number card to the class counting strip and fill in the next number on the blank 200 chart.

Materials

- Prepared set of large Yektti Picture Cards (1 set for class)
- Prepared set of Small Yektti Picture Cards (1 set per group)
- Prepared set of Yektti Word Cards (1 set per group)
- Student Sheet 3 (1 per student, homework)

Activity

Read the following story to start off this session.

All About Yekttis

A Strange Discovery

Amanda and Ari, eight-year-old twins, discovered some strange creatures near their home in Wyoming. These creatures were living in abandoned prairie dog burrows next to a dirt road that the twins used as a shortcut to school. Amanda and Ari started studying these creatures. They visited them every chance they had. Because these creatures never came all the way out of their holes in the ground, Amanda and Ari could see only their heads. The creatures looked as though they might have come from another planet.

Ari loved to make up codes and learn about languages. After a few months, he learned how to say some words in the creatures' own language,

and he taught them a few words in English and in Spanish. He learned that the creatures called themselves Yekttis (YEK-tees), that they came from a very distant planet, and that they were peaceful.

Amanda liked to study different kinds of living things. She decided to do a report about the Yekttis for a science project at school. She made a sketch of the head of each of the Yekttis she had seen. She noticed that a lot of them were similar to one another but that no two were exactly alike. She used her sketches to figure out how she could describe to other human beings what the Yekttis looked like.

❖ **Tip for the Linguistically Diverse Classroom** To make this story comprehensible for students with limited English proficiency, volunteers can act out parts such as discovering the creatures, learning to say some words in the creatures' language, and teaching them Spanish and English. As students act out the story, draw sketches on the chalkboard to convey key words (*prairie dog, burrows, school*) that will not be comprehensible in the enactment.

Describing the Yekttis Using the set of Large Yektti Cards, show the class a picture of just one Yektti.

Today we will look at copies of Amanda's sketches, then try to describe the Yekttis.

I'm going to show you some Yekttis, one at a time. Here's the first one. What can you tell me about what a Yektti looks like? Here's another Yektti. What do you see that's the same as or that's different from the first one? Remember, Amanda and Ari found out that the Yekttis were similar, but no two were exactly alike.

Gradually reveal more Yektti Cards as students develop their descriptions. Challenge students to figure out the special attributes of these creatures. See the **Teacher Note,** About the Yekttis (p. 29), for more information about their attributes.

You've seen quite a few of the Yekttis, and you've made some observations about how they look. Now can you describe a particular Yektti that you think I might have a card for? Juanita said that this one has a square head and three antennae. Can anyone think of another one I might have that's like this one but not exactly like it?

To stress the informational nature of each student's contributions, rather than whether a particular description is "correct," respond to each description with another piece of information. For example, a student might ask, "Do you have a Yektti with a square head and five antennae?" You could respond, "No, I don't have one with five antennae, but I have this square one with four antennae." For further ideas, see the **Dialogue Box,** Describing the Set of Yekttis (p. 30).

At first, students may have difficulty concentrating on more than one attribute at a time. Choose Yekttis with the same head shape until students have begun to realize that there are different eye types and different numbers of antennae. As students are feeling comfortable with the information they have deduced so far, introduce new head shapes dramatically!

Keep the Yekttis students have identified along the chalkboard ledge or held up by students standing in front of the group, while the class tries to figure out which ones they haven't yet identified.

Through questioning, students gradually infer the attributes of the Yekttis: the four head shapes, the four numbers of antennae, and the two eye types. After a while, you can ask students to specify completely all three attributes of the Yektti they want to see, "I want a triangle Yektti with one antenna and ringed eyes."

Students often come up with their own descriptive vocabulary, especially to describe the Yekttis' eyes. Some have called the plain eyes "cookie eyes" or "hamburger eyes" and the ringed eyes "doughnut eyes" or "bagel eyes." Using students' invented words for these descriptions is fine. The eyes are called plain and ringed on the game cards used in the next activity; eventually you will need to establish this common vocabulary.

When the discussion has touched on all the possible Yektti types, ask students to summarize the attributes of Yekttis. They can list attributes that all Yekttis have (a mouth, no nose, no ears) and attributes that differ (the four head shapes, the two eye types, and the number of antennae ranging from one to four). There is no need to generate descriptions of all thirty-two of the individual Yekttis, but some classes do enjoy figuring out every one.

Teacher Checkpoint

Guess My Rule with Yektti Cards

Teacher Checkpoints are places for you to stop and observe student work. For more information on how to use Teacher Checkpoints, see About Assessment (p. I-10).

Divide the class into groups of three or four and give each group Small Yektti Picture Cards and Yektti Word Cards. For the remainder of this session, students play Guess My Rule with the Yektti Cards.

We have been playing Guess My Rule with students in our class. Today you will play Guess My Rule with the Yektti Cards. You will need a set of Yektti Picture Cards and a set of Yektti Word Cards. The word cards describe the Yekttis.

Go through the set of word cards to make sure students can identify the different attributes described on them. Then explain that group members will take turns deciding on a mystery rule about the Yektti Picture Cards (for example, Yekttis with plain eyes or Yekttis with three antennae). A student can either think of a rule and then find the word card that matches it, or simply select a card. The word card describing the mystery rule should be placed face down on a flat surface. The word cards are useful reminders if a student forgets which rule was chosen and serve to reassure the guessers that there is a clear rule.

❖ **Tip for the Linguistically Diverse Classroom** Students with limited English proficiency may need additional help in understanding the attributes described on the word cards. These students can draw pictures to illustrate the words on their sets of cards.

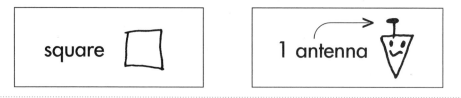

Next, the Yektti Picture Cards are arranged on a flat surface. The student picks out a Yektti Picture Card or two to start the game, saying something like, "These Yekttis fit my rule." Other group members take turns asking if a particular Yektti fits. If it fits, the picture card is placed in the center of the playing area. If it doesn't fit, the card is placed to one side.

When you are playing Guess My Rule, remember that the Yektti Picture Cards that don't fit the mystery rule have important information on them. Make a separate group for these cards. By looking at all the information, you can get a better idea of what the mystery rule might be.

You may need to remind groups several times that they should try to figure out the mystery rule by choosing picture cards that represent examples of the rule, not by just guessing different rules. Only when it seems that most group members have figured out the mystery rule, or when most of the cards have been placed, can they guess what the rule is. Then the rule maker can turn over the word card to confirm it. Some groups like to have all cards placed before the rule is revealed. Each group member should have at least one turn choosing the mystery rule.

Observing the Students For some, this game will be easy. However, this is the first time students will be playing Guess My Rule on their own in small groups. In addition to observing carefully the classification of the cards, students will be struggling with taking turns and—when it's their turn to choose the rule—managing others' guesses, giving accurate feedback, and deciding at what point players can guess the rule. For students who are just beginning to learn about group collaboration, this is all hard work. As you circulate, participate briefly in each group's game so that you can continue to model the need for careful observation of both positive and negative evidence. Where appropriate, help students decide on ways to manage their group work.

At this point, some groups may invent the "double rule" game that you will be introducing in the next activity. Encourage them to experiment with two rules if they are ready.

Sessions 4 and 5 Follow-Up

 **Homework**

Today's Number   After Session 4, have students record today's number in the blank on Student Sheet 3, Today's Number. For homework, students think of five ways to make today's number and record their solutions on the student sheet. They may use any operation and as many numbers as they wish. Students may ask a family member to think of a sixth way.

Extensions

How Many in All?   Before distributing Small Yektti Picture Cards to groups, present the following problem: "Yekttis are fantasy creatures from outer space. They have from one to four antennae, two kinds of eyes, and four head shapes. There is one Yektti for every possible way you could put these things together. No two Yektti look exactly alike. How many Yekttis are there in all?" Many second graders have been able to make pictures or diagrams to figure out the solution.

Using the Computer for Classification

- *Tabletop Jr.*   *Tabletop Jr.* is a computer environment that engages primary students in grouping, sorting, and classifying data; collecting and organizing information; and graphing and interpreting data. Students can create free-form arrangements of data or they can organize data using bunches, Venn diagrams, and simple bar graphs, as well as other types of grids and graphs. *Tabletop Jr.* offers students a variety of data sets including a set of Yekttis they can organize and represent. In addition, students can create their own data sets, which they then can choose to organize in various ways.

  Tabletop Jr. by Broderbund is available from Dale Seymour Publications. Hardware requirements are:

  > Apple Macintosh version: LC, II, Centris, or equivalent; Apple System 6.0.8 or higher; 2 MB RAM; 256-color monitor
  >
  > or
  >
  > Microsoft Windows versions 386SX or higher; Windows 3.1; 4MB RAM; VGA

- *Gertrude's Secrets*   *Gertrude's Secrets,* software from The Learning Company, contains three types of classification games. The loop puzzles are a version of Guess My Rule using shape and color. Students may like to use the Shape Editing Room, in which they make their own shapes to use in puzzles. *Gertrude's Secrets* runs on Apple 2GS computers.

About the Yekttis

Yekttis (YEK-tees) are fantasy creatures from outer space. They have from one to four antennae, two types of eyes (ringed or plain), and four head shapes (square, triangle, rhombus, or hexagon). The Yektti Cards are a set of attribute cards; that is, a set of cards that can be sorted and classified according to the characteristics of the set. Like other attribute materials, this set is structured so that there is one Yektti with each possible combination of characteristics; for example, there is one triangular Yektti with three antennae and ringed eyes, one triangular Yektti with three antennae and plain eyes, one square Yektti with three antennae and plain eyes, and so on.

Unlike most sets of related things in the real world, the Yektti set has only three attributes (number of antennae, head shape, eye type). Students have already dealt with a more complex set—themselves—that has endless possibilities for classification, and later in this unit they will be developing their own categories for groups of things with much less well-defined characteristics. However, attribute materials like the Yekttis are useful exactly because they are more limited. Because the Yekttis can be sorted into only a few categories that can be easily deduced, students can concentrate on making careful observations and reasoning from evidence. In this investigation, students engage in sorting activities that require them to take into account more than one attribute at a time. The Yekttis help students learn about more complex sorting in a context that is not too overwhelming.

A complete Yektti Card set contains 32 individual Yekttis, one with each possible combination of head shape, eye type, and number of antennae. For this investigation, you will need one set of Large Yektti Picture Cards for class use and sets of Small Yektti Picture Cards for each small group.

For whole-class work, you will need only the Large Yektti Picture Cards. Some teachers have made transparencies of them for use on an overhead projector. For small-group work, each group will need its own set of Small Yektti Picture Cards and a set of Yektti Word Cards.

Working with sorting materials such as attribute block sets (sometimes called A-blocks), logic blocks, or game pieces is an appropriate extension throughout this unit. The game Guess My Rule, as well as many other activities in which students investigate classification, can be done with these materials. Attribute materials are sets of blocks or drawings on cards that vary in shape, color, size, or other characteristics. The Yekttis in this unit are one version of attribute material. Another is the set of 32 attribute blocks developed by Elementary Science Study. Four colors, four shapes, and two sizes are represented in the set, and there is one block for each possible combination of characteristics (for example, one big yellow triangle, one small blue square). These are available from most distributors of mathematical manipulatives.

☐ D I A L O G U E ☐ B O X ☐

Describing the Set of Yekttis

In this discussion, which takes place during the activity All About Yekttis (p. 23), students are describing the attributes of various Yekttis shown on large picture cards.

Here is one of the Yekttis. Can you figure out how Yekttis look?

Students: It looks like a triangle . . . It has antennae . . . It has big eyes . . . It has doughnut eyes . . . It has rings around it . . . Like a bagel . . . It has a small mouth.

These are good descriptions. Let me show you another Yektti.

Students: The eyes look like cookies . . . The mouth looks like a worm . . . It has only one antenna.

What did the other one have?

Juanita: Three.

I'll show you another one.

Bjorn: It only has two antennae.

Franco: I see a pattern. The first one had three—3, 2, 1! The next one probably has four.

I do have one with four antennae. Here it is. Can anyone describe another Yektti I might have here?

Ebony: Do you have one with doughnut eyes?

I do. Here it is. Who can ask for another one?

Graham: One with four antennae.

I do have some with four antennae, but can you tell me more about the one you want?

Graham: And cookie eyes.

I do have one like that. Here it is. [*Shows one with a square head.*] Who can describe another Yektti?

Imani: A square one with three antennae?

Yes. Actually I have two different square ones with three antennae. Can you tell me anything else about the one you want?

Imani: It has doughnut eyes!

Tory: A round one with three antennae?

No, I don't have any round ones, but I do have some other Yekttis with three antennae, like this one. [*Shows a hexagon head with plain eyes and three antennae.*] This shape is called a hexagon. It has six sides. You're the first person to figure out something that's not true about Yekttis, Tory. Who thinks he or she can tell me about a different hexagon Yektti?

Trini: A hexagon with one antenna.

Can you give me a little more information?

Trini: With cookie eyes.

[*Later*]

Simon: A diamond Yektti with one antenna and plain eyes.

Yes, I have one like that. Here it is. That was a careful description. I knew exactly which one you meant. Who else can look carefully and tell me all the information I need for another one that's not out yet?

Olga: The same but with three horns.

The same?

Olga: Yes, a diamond with cookie eyes like the other one, but with three horns . . . no, we have that one already. With two horns.

Paul: And a four—the same with four antennae.

Olga: It's like a family.

Harris: Can I ask a question? How come they probably get older and older and grow more antennae, like one and then they get two?

Ayaz: Yes, maybe it's the baby with just one antenna.

Temara: Or maybe the babies are born bald, but they stay underground, so you never see them unless they're old enough to have one antenna.

Introducing Venn Diagrams

What Happens

Students are introduced to Venn diagrams as a way of representing data that have been sorted. They play Guess My Rule with Yektti Picture Cards, using two attributes. They organize and represent the data using a Venn diagram. Their work focuses on:

- considering two attributes at one time
- using a Venn diagram to organize data

Start-Up

Today's Number   Sometime during the school day, students brainstorm ways to express Today's Number using three addends. For example, if Today's Number is 68, possible responses include: 30 + 30 + 8 or 20 + 20 + 28. Add a card to the class counting strip and fill in the next number on the blank 200 chart.

Materials

- Prepared Diagram A (1 for class)
- Prepared Diagram B (1 per group)
- Small Yektti Picture Cards (1 set per group)
- Yektti Word Cards (1 set per group and extras)
- Yarn or string (optional)
- Student Sheet 4 (1 per student, homework)

Representing Two Attributes

For information about the Venn diagrams you will be using in this session, see the **Teacher Note,** Venn Diagrams: Sorting by Two Attributes (p. 34). Have students gather around you on the floor or a table where you have placed the large sheet of paper with two nonoverlapping circles on it. (Diagram A as described on p. 3.) Choose two Yektti Word Cards—for example, SQUARE and 2 ANTENNAE. Place the cards face down, one in each circle.

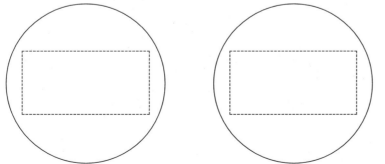

Play Guess My Rule using a set of Small Yektti Picture Cards. Students specify in which circle a card should be placed. Cards that do not fit either rule can be placed in a visible space—for example, around the edges of the circles.

As students play, they will be faced with the problem of where to put the Yekttis that have both attributes. Encourage all students' suggestions. For example, students might suggest a third circle that shows square Yekttis with two antennae, or placing the cards that fit both rules so that the cards touch both circles. Once students guess the mystery rule, turn over the Yektti Word Cards and continue the sorting.

After completing one game, display the large paper with two overlapping circles (Diagram B as described on p. 3). Or, if you are using string or yarn to portray the diagram, move the loops so that they overlap.

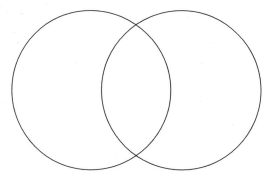

These overlapping circles make a Venn diagram. You can use the name Venn diagram, or you can call it a circle diagram. A Venn diagram is a picture that mathematicians use to solve the problem of things that belong in two groups. The special place in the middle is really inside both circles, so that's where the Yekttis that are square and have two antennae can go. Which ones should we move to the middle?

After they sort all the cards, ask students to describe what they see.

Which Yekttis can go only in the left circle? How did you figure that out? Which can go only in the right circle? When did you guess that was the rule? Which go in the middle? What kinds of Yekttis can't go in either of the circles? (Yekttis that are hexagons, triangles, and diamonds with 1, 3, or 4 antennae) **How do you know?**

Many kinds of analytic skills are involved in this investigation. Some students will be able to place the Yektti cards accurately but may not be able to verbalize the descriptions of each group. Others may be able to describe the groups once they are formed but may not be as good at using evidence to classify the cards during the course of the game. Students will learn from one another throughout these activities.

Try one or two more rounds of the game, using the intersecting circles, before students break up into their small groups.

Sorting by Two Rules

Divide the class into groups of three or four students. Groups play Guess My Rule with two mystery rules, using Diagram B, Small Yektti Picture Cards, and Yektti Word Cards. The rule maker will choose two word cards, one for each circle. As you circulate, remind students that the middle section of the diagram is really inside both circles and is the place for Yekttis that fit both rules. If one circle is for triangles and the other is for plain eyes, Yekttis with triangle heads and plain eyes fit in the intersection. Sometimes no Yekttis will fit in the middle. For example, a Yektti can't have both a triangular and a hexagonal head. However, it is still perfectly legitimate to use these two attributes as rules.

Continue to circulate and support students as they become increasingly independent in managing their group work and thinking about these difficult classification problems. Some students, using the game playing from the previous activity as a model, will begin to discuss their strategies. See the **Dialogue Box,** How Did You Know? (p. 35), for examples of strategies used by students. With your own questioning, encourage other students to begin to discuss how they are thinking about the problems.

Session 6 Follow-Up

Yektti Stories   This is an ideal activity to integrate with writing and art. For homework, students will write a story about the Yekttis. They might also want to draw a picture of what they think a whole Yektti looks like. Since only the Yekttis' heads have been seen, it is anybody's guess what their bodies look like! According to the Yektti story, Ari did learn to communicate with the Yekttis a little. However, their language was very strange and difficult, so he couldn't ask them a lot of the questions that he wanted to. He didn't find out why they never came out of the holes in the ground or what the rest of their bodies looked like. You may want to discuss these or other similar questions with your students in preparation for the homework: What do they eat? Do they work? If so, doing what? Do they live in families? What do they do for fun? What is their home planet like? Students record their stories and illustrations on Student Sheet 4, Yektti Stories.

Guess My Rule with Words   Using students' spelling words or any set of word cards, small groups can play Guess My Rule with words. Rules such as HAS AN E, STARTS WITH S, HAS DOUBLE LETTERS, and HAS TWO VOWELS could be used. This also works well as a chalkboard game with the class when you have a few minutes to fill before lunch or at the end of the school day.

Other Attribute Materials   See the **Teacher Note,** About the Yekttis (p. 29), for a discussion of appropriate attribute materials to use for further classification activities.

MURDOCK LEARNING RESOURCE CENTER

To introduce Venn diagrams, begin with two nonoverlapping circles, so that students can think about two rules at a time and invent ways of dealing with items that fit in both categories.

Suppose students are sorting animals according to two categories: ANIMALS THAT LIVE IN THE NEIGHBORHOOD and ANIMALS THAT CAN HOP. They might think of these animals:

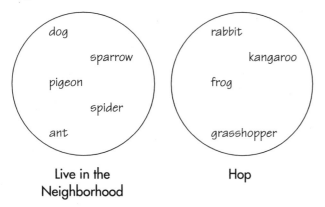

Students soon realize that some of the animals fit in both circles. Suppose that in the neighborhood there aren't any rabbits or kangaroos, but there are grasshoppers and frogs. You could write these animals in both circles, or you might place them above and between the two circles.

However, mathematicians have a way of representing the data that clearly show the relationship between the two categories. Moving the two circles together creates an overlapping space that is inside both circles. Now it can be seen that some animals fit in only one circle, some fit in only the other circle, and some fit in both:

The word *and* is important in describing the space inside the two circles, which can be referred to as the overlap or intersection. The grasshopper and frog hop *and* live in the neighborhood. The animals in the circle on the left live in the neighborhood but do not hop. The animals in the circle on the right hop but do not live in the neighborhood.

Some teachers emphasize the separate categories by drawing the two circles in different colors or making them with two different colors of ribbon or string. Color provides an easy way to identify each circle: "Does this one fit in the yellow circle?" "Are you ready to guess the rule for the blue circle?" "Everything in the yellow circle has two antennae."

Even though a space exists for items that fit in both categories, there may not be any such items. For example, if your two categories are BROWN EYES and BLUE EYES, no students fit both criteria. This situation will come up in using the Yekttis when students select two word cards, such as *square* and *hexagon,* that describe two mutually exclusive categories. That is, no Yektti has a square head *and* a hexagon head.

This situation might also arise in classifying real data. Suppose you are classifying animals in two categories: ANIMALS THAT LIVE IN THE NEIGHBORHOOD and ANIMALS THAT SWIM. In one community there might be no animals that fit in the intersection:

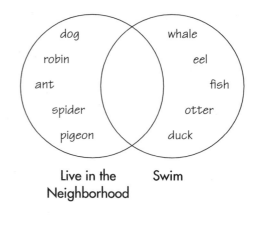

Continued on next page

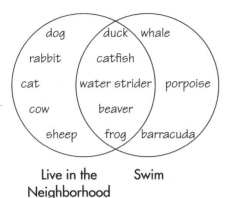

dog
rabbit
cat
cow
sheep

duck
catfish
water strider
beaver
frog

whale
porpoise
barracuda

Live in the
Neighborhood   Swim

In another community, there might be many animals that fit in the intersection.

In this second case, the duck, catfish, water strider, beaver, and frog all live in the neighborhood *and* swim.

D I A L O G U E   B O X

How Did You Know?

Jeffrey, Ebony, Ayaz, and Olga are playing Guess My Rule. Jeffrey has chosen two Yektti Word Cards: RINGED EYES and TRIANGLE. In this discussion during the activity Sorting by Two Rules (p. 33), the other students are trying to guess Jeffrey's mystery rules.

Ebony: [*Chooses four antennae, ringed eyes, square*] Does this fit the rule?

Jeffrey: Yes, it goes here.

Ayaz: [*Picks four antennae, ringed eyes, hexagon*] This one?

Jeffrey: Yes.

Ayaz: Oh, it could be two of one, I mean one of two. They both have doughnut eyes and they both have four antennae.

Olga: [*Holds up four antennae, ringed eyes, diamond*] This one goes.

Ayaz: But it could still be both.

Ebony: [*Shows four antennae, plain eyes, diamond*] I know! This one!

Jeffrey: No, it's a reject. Good information!

[*Ayaz silently holds up a three antennae, ringed eyes, diamond Yektti.*]

Jeffrey: It fits.

Ebony: Can I guess it? [*Jeffrey nods.*] It's RINGED EYES.

Olga: How did you know?

Ebony: I looked over here [*indicates the discards*] and I saw there were no RINGED EYES.

Ayaz: At first I thought it was FOUR ANTENNAE, but that one [*points to four antennae, plain eyes*] didn't go, so I changed my mind.

Olga: This is good. You got it after eleven cards.

Jeffrey: But you don't know my other rule yet.

Collections: What Goes Together?

What Happens

Sessions 1 and 2: Exploring Thing Collections
Using a collection of common objects, students
explore and identify physical attributes of these
objects that they can see and feel, such as what
the object is made of or what color it is. They sort
objects into groups and try to identify the attribute
that unifies the objects in a particular group. In
small groups they play Guess My Rule.

Sessions 3 and 4: Sink and Float   Students collect
data about whether objects in their Thing
Collections sink or float when placed in water. In
small groups they organize the experiment, collect
and record the data, organize the data, and then
make a representation of their organization.
Based on their findings, students pose hypotheses
about the properties of objects that sink and
objects that float.

Mathematical Emphasis

- Thinking flexibly about the characteristics of
  data
- Articulating logical reasoning
- Constructing categories with clear definitions
  for describing categorical data
- Inventing representations of data
- Using more than one representation to view
  data
- Building theories about the data

Note: This investigation can be easily integrated
with the science curriculum, and you may want to
add some experiments in line with science activities you are planning. See the Extensions at the
end of Sessions 3 and 4 for suggestions.

What to Plan Ahead of Time

Materials

- Chart paper (Sessions 1–2)
- Index cards: about 45 plus extras (Sessions 1–2)
- Overhead projector (Sessions 1–2, optional)
- Yarn or string (Sessions 1–2, optional)
- Assorted small objects such as beads, buttons, paper cups, and sponges for Thing Collections: about 10–15 of each (Sessions 1–4)
- Resealable plastic bags: about 15 (Sessions 1–4)
- Tubs or basins: about 10 (Sessions 3–4)
- Large sheets of paper: about 20 (Sessions 3–4)
- Sheets of newspaper (Sessions 3–4, optional)

Other Preparation

- Duplicate student sheets and teaching resources (located at the end of this unit) in the following quantities. If you have Student Activity Booklets, copy only the transparency marked with an asterisk.

For Sessions 1–2

Student Sheet 5, Guess My Rule with Thing Collections (p. 140): 1 per student (homework)

One-circle diagram (p. 142): 1 per group of 2–3 students. Make a transparency* of the one-circle diagram or draw a large circle on chart paper or shape one out of yarn.

For Sessions 3–4

Student Sheet 6, Playing Guess My Rule with Thing Collections (p. 141): 1 per student (homework)

- Prepare identical Thing Collections of about 20 small objects—one collection for each group of 2–3 students and an extra for yourself. Store each in a resealable plastic bag. See the **Teacher Note,** Preparing a Thing Collection (p. 43), for specific suggestions. (Sessions 1–2)

- Set up a small tub or basin half-filled with water for each group of 2–3 students. Plastic washing tubs work well. Borrow tubs from the science or the kindergarten teachers, or ask students to bring tubs from home. The tubs should be on a surface that can get wet and be wiped off later. Spread newspapers on the floor under the tubs. (Sessions 3–4)

- For objects in the Thing Collections that are likely to disintegrate or get waterlogged, such as index cards, have extras available so students will be able to try these items more than once. (Sessions 3–4)

Exploring Thing Collections

Materials

- Thing Collections (1 per group)
- One-circle diagram (1 per group)
- Chart paper
- Index cards (about 3 per group)
- One-circle diagram (on a transparency or chart paper)
- Overhead projector (optional)
- Yarn or string (optional)
- Student Sheet 5 (1 per student, homework)

What Happens

Using a collection of common objects, students explore and identify physical attributes of these objects that they can see and feel, such as what the object is made of or what color it is. They sort objects into groups and try to identify the attribute that unifies the objects in a particular group. In small groups they play Guess My Rule. Their work focuses on:

- sorting and grouping objects according to similar attributes
- developing and defining categories based on physical attributes
- identifying a common attribute for a group of objects
- using negative information to identify how objects are sorted

Start-Up

Today's Number Sometime during the school day, students brainstorm ways to express the number of days they have been in school. Suggest that they include subtraction in each number sentence. For example, if Today's Number is 69, possible solutions include: 70 – 1 or 100 – 31. Add a card to the class counting strip and fill in another number on the blank 200 chart.

Activity

Exploring the Collections

Distribute a Thing Collection to each group of 2–3 students. Allow about 10 minutes for students to look through their collections. Encourage students to touch, look closely, count, sort, or use any other mode of exploration.

Many groups will be able to manage their own exploration. For any group that needs help focusing, suggest one of the following:

- After everyone has had a chance to look carefully at the materials, one student holds the collection in its container on his or her lap (out of sight) while the others try to name as many objects in the collection as they can.
- With the collection in sight, play Twenty Questions to guess which object one student has in mind.

After students have had a chance to examine their collections, gather the groups together.

You've been learning to look carefully as you think about what's the same and what's different in a group of things. You did this when we played Guess My Rule with the class and with the Yekttis. Now can you tell me what's the same and what's different about all the things in your collection?

Encourage students to make statements about the whole collection, not just about individual objects. See the **Teacher Note,** Making Generalizations About a Thing Collection (p. 44), for suggestions that will help students clarify their statements. This discussion is an introduction to the collections, giving students a chance to observe carefully and to use and hear a variety of words that describe the objects. Allow about 5–10 minutes for this discussion.

Record students' descriptions of the collections and organize their information in a chart.

This collection does:	This collection does not:
have 20 objects	have anything alive
have some shiny things	have anything green
have a lot of small things	

or

Everything in the collection:	is metal, plastic, or paper is smaller than a chalkboard eraser is larger than a penny
Nothing in the collection:	is alive can be eaten is gold or silver
Some things in the collection:	are white are round you can write on are useful

Guess My Rule: Thing Collections

We're going to play Guess My Rule with the collections. It may be harder now than when we played it with the Yekttis, because there are a lot more possible rules. Look carefully at everything and don't guess too quickly. You should be able to give good reasons for your ideas.

Give each group a one-circle diagram. Put a transparency with a large circle on the overhead, or draw a large circle on chart paper, or make one out of yarn. Gather students together in an area where they all can see.

This is a one-circle diagram. We're going to play with only one rule at a time today. When we find a thing that fits the rule, we'll put it inside the circle. When we find a thing that doesn't fit, we'll put it outside the circle.

Depending on the things in your collections, a good beginning mystery rule may be ROUND. Start students off by telling them one or two objects that go inside the circle and one or two that belong outside the circle. As objects that fit or don't fit are identified, ask students to follow along, using their own collections and circle diagrams. Demonstrate how to place the objects using the overhead projector (or using the chart paper or yarn circles).

As students make guesses, challenge them to consider all the evidence, both negative and positive. Since students now have prior experience with Guess My Rule, you should no longer need to accept all conjectures as equally legitimate. Begin to ask students to give reasons for their ideas. See the **Teacher Note,** Mathematical Discussions: Challenging Ideas (p. 45), and the **Dialogue Box,** Paying Attention to the Evidence (p. 48), for questioning techniques to use with students.

Play the game one more time, perhaps using METAL or PAPER as your rule.

Describing the Collections

Students now play Guess My Rule in small groups, using their Thing Collections and one-circle diagrams. As students are playing, circulate around the room, helping them to clarify the rules they are using and encouraging them to find words that accurately describe their rule.

Encourage each student in the group to have a turn thinking of a mystery rule. You may need to remind students that instead of randomly guessing rules they should test their ideas by asking the leader whether an object fits inside (or outside) the circle. In this way the game is extended and students collect more information to back up or disprove their ideas.

Creating Sorting Rules

Near the end of Session 2, each small group chooses one mystery rule about their Thing Collection and challenges the rest of the class in a round of Guess My Rule. Before play begins, each group writes its rule on an index card and sorts its collection according to that rule. This process will help each group clearly define the rule.

If you have an overhead projector, students enjoy using it with the one-circle diagram as the other groups follow along with their own collections. As in the previous session, challenge students to clarify and defend their conjectures. This investigation provides many opportunities for language experiences and enriching vocabulary. See the **Teacher Note,** Using Fancy Words (p. 46), for examples of describing words students use.

You can also organize this activity by having groups visit each other's collection and try to guess the mystery rule. One way to do this is, after groups have sorted their collections, have half of the them visit another group and guess their rule, then switch roles.

As students try to guess each other's mystery rules, you will notice some of the difficulties inherent in describing a real-world collection with so many different attributes. The **Teacher Note,** The Challenge of Fuzzy Attributes: The Teacher's Role (p. 46), offers some suggestions for dealing with them. It is appropriate for students to struggle with these difficulties; they are real problems that come up in describing real data. Continue to encourage students to refer to the characteristics of the objects for evidence.

❖ **Tip for the Linguistically Diverse Classroom** As an aid for students with limited English proficiency, encourage the class to point to specific attributes of objects and pantomime motions as they express their mystery rules.

Sessions 1 and 2 Follow-Up

🏠 Homework

Guess My Rule with Thing Collections Students assemble their own Thing Collections using objects from around their homes. They use their collections to play Guess My Rule with family members. Students should play at least two rounds of Guess My Rule and make a list of the objects in their collections on Student Sheet 5, Guess My Rule with Thing Collections. Remind students to keep their collections in a safe place, as they will need them again.

〽 Extensions

Guess My Rule: Two Rules Students can use the collections to play Guess My Rule with two sorting rules. Give each group a diagram of overlapping circles (Diagram B from Investigation 1), and index cards for this game. Because the Thing Collections, unlike the Yekttis, can be sorted in so many different ways, playing Guess My Rule using two sorting rules can be quite challenging. As students play, remind them that one rule applies to one circle, the second rule to the other circle, and that objects in the intersection are in both circles and, therefore, must fit both rules. The rule maker should write the two mystery rules on index cards and place them face down near the two circles before the game begins. This activity is excellent for independent group work or for a learning center.

Making Classroom Collections Each pair or small group of students creates its own collection of objects based on a characteristic they choose. In previous experiences, students have chosen such attributes as THINGS MADE OUT OF METAL, THINGS THAT ARE RED, JUNK FOOD, and THINGS YOU CAN'T BREAK.

An alternative is to choose one or two attributes and have the whole class bring in objects. The attributes might relate to other curriculum areas—for example, THINGS THAT CAN BE PICKED UP BY A MAGNET, THINGS THAT USED TO BE ALIVE, THINGS THAT DON'T COME FROM THE UNITED STATES, or THINGS THAT BIRDS WILL EAT.

Even simple attributes can be interesting. One classroom brought in THINGS THAT ARE BLUE and made a display of objects with an amazing range of blues. Even here, definition and description were challenging: Do we all agree on what is blue? Does blue include purple? When does blue shade off into green? What are other words that describe some shade of blue?

Preparing a Thing Collection

Collections of common objects give students the chance to explore similarities and differences in shape, color, texture, material, function, and a variety of other properties. Following are a few guidelines for putting together classroom Thing Collections.

■ A collection of about 20 small objects provides enough variety and is a manageable size for second graders.

■ As you choose objects, look for a few clear properties that are shared by four to eight objects. For example, you might include seven round things, five red things, six metal things, and four plastic things. Some objects might have more than one of these characteristics.

■ Try to avoid too much variety in color so students will focus on other properties.

■ You will need some objects that will sink and some that will float in water. Also include a few things that float for a while, then sink once they become waterlogged (index card), or things that sometimes sink and sometimes float, depending on how you put them into the water (paper cup).

■ Because you will be playing Guess My Rule with the whole class, and each small group will be using its own collection, all the collections should be identical. For instance, if you include pipe cleaners, put the same colors in each collection. If you include paper clips, use the same size for everyone.

■ Store each collection in a resealable plastic bag. (Sometimes students count the container as part of the collection, too.)

■ You may want to exclude things that roll easily (like marbles) because they are hard to sort on flat surfaces.

■ Keep a supply of duplicate objects, as some will inevitably be lost or broken, or will disintegrate when put in water.

You will probably have your own ideas for suitable objects that are readily available. A list of suggested items is given here.

index card
pipe cleaner
button
small paper clip
large paper clip
red checker
black checker
birthday candle
piece of sponge
plastic coffee can lid
drinking straw
rubber band
piece of string
peanut (in the shell)
sugar cube
piece of dry pasta
plastic drink stirrer
interlocking cube
craft stick (or tongue depressor)
piece of aluminum foil
jack
key
screw
toothpick
wooden bead
paper cup
penny
paint brush
pencil
tile
marker top

Making Generalizations About a Thing Collection

Looking at a Thing Collection as a whole is a difficult task for many second graders. Students at this level are often used to focusing on individual objects and individual characteristics. However, at this point in the unit, they have had some good experience in making generalizations about a group by focusing on one particular characteristic and ignoring others. For example, when they played Guess My Rule with the class, they described one group as WEARING BLUE and ignored everything else that was different about the individuals in that group.

Teachers have found that it is sometimes hard to get the initial discussion going. But once students hear a few examples, they quickly catch on to the idea of making general statements about the collection. For example, characteristics of the collections that students have noticed include:

Some of it is little and some of it is big.

Most of it isn't made out of paper.

There are some things you can stir with.

Some things have spirals.

They're not alive.

Nothing is gold.

You can see through some of the things.

The particular characteristics your students see will depend on the objects in your collection.

As students offer their generalizations, encourage them to clarify what they mean. For instance, one student's remark that "you can see through some things" prompted a discussion of what she meant by "see through." As it turned out, she meant transparent, but some students pointed out that they could "see through" a wooden bead in the collection because it had a hole in the middle.

When another student suggested that "most of it isn't made out of paper," the teacher asked her to clarify what she meant by "most." The students found that three objects (out of twenty) were made of paper and agreed that, therefore, "most" objects were not paper. Another student suggested that "some are big and some are small," and the teacher asked everyone to talk about which objects they would call big or small and why.

You will certainly have ideas about how you would describe the collection. However, it is more important that students clarify their own thinking and express their own ideas precisely than that they agree with your descriptions.

Mathematical Discussions: Challenging Ideas ⟨ Teacher Note

One of the most important ideas in mathematics is that one's assertions should be subject to scrutiny and challenge. The history of mathematics is the history of debate and discussion, yet we do not see much discussion in most mathematics classes.

In fact, many students are convinced that there is always one "right" answer and one "best" procedure in mathematics class. This idea often leads them to be nervous if their answers or strategies seem to conflict. But discussion about different strategies, different approaches, and different solutions lies at the heart of mathematics. Encouraging students to make assertions, to base their arguments on data, to state their reasons, and to ask others clarifying questions are vital aspects of teaching mathematics.

Challenging students' ideas is a delicate matter, yet it can be a very effective way of probing what students are thinking and helping them clarify and extend their own ideas. Many teachers find that the best way of examining students' ideas is to ask questions that invite them to explain their reasons:

Say more about that. Can you give me an example? How do the data tell you that?

Another technique is to ask students to relate their ideas to other students' ideas:

Is this like Laura's idea? Are your reasons the same as Graham's? Juanita's idea and Jeffrey's are very different. Could they both work? What would help us know if either of these ideas works?

A third way teachers sometimes probe students' ideas is to give counterexamples or suggest thought experiments:

Some other second graders say that heavy things always sink. What would you tell them? Do you think anything would change if we collected more data from other second graders? Do you think if we asked the same questions again today, the answers would be the same as they were yesterday?

You may have other techniques that work for you. Once ideas are flowing, you may find that the students themselves make many suggestions, ask each other probing questions, and help to formulate ideas. Until then, however, it is important to keep discussion alive. Researchers have found that simply waiting three seconds after asking a question gives students time to organize their thinking and to develop some of their ideas before answering. Three seconds seems like a very long time when you're used to much faster answers, but students need to feel that they have time to think. Hurrying them to an answer defeats the whole purpose of mathematical discussions.

Using Fancy Words

This investigation is a particularly good one for integrating language experience and vocabulary development into mathematics. As students struggle to describe the characteristics of their collections, they hear new words from other students, and you can find opportunities to introduce other words that are appropriate to the conversation. Students in the primary grades enjoy learning and using "fancy words" when they are embedded in some compelling experience rather than isolated as vocabulary words to be memorized.

For example, one student said that some objects were "like glass." Once the teacher clarified what the student meant, she introduced the word *transparent* into the conversation ("Oh, you mean it's transparent, you can see right through it?")—not insisting that students use this word, but simply adding it to the vocabulary they were hearing. Not surprisingly, many students began to use the word as they continued the investigation.

A small group that chose THINGS THAT ARE HALFWAY TO A CIRCLE (including a paper clip and a craft stick) expressed beautifully, using words they understood, the idea of semicircular. The teacher acknowledged the students' definition by repeating their wording and also offered them new vocabulary: "Oh, things that are halfway to a circle, I see exactly what you mean. There's a half circle—you can call it a *semicircle*—right here on the paper clip, and there are semicircles on the ends of the craft stick."

Malleable, unbreakable, and *opaque* are other "fancy" words that have surfaced in classrooms during this investigation.

The Challenge of Fuzzy Attributes: The Teacher's Role

Work with the Thing Collections is quite different from work with the Yekttis. The Thing Collections provide experience with the real problems that arise in classifying data. As in many other real-world data sets, the number of different attributes of objects in the collections is almost limitless. Further, many of the attributes are "fuzzy," not as easy to define clearly as those of the Yekttis. There is no disagreement about whether a Yektti has one or two antennae, but there is room for discussion about which objects in the collection are useful or small or long. Some rules students have invented include:

> THINGS YOU CAN TIE
>
> THINGS THAT ARE HALFWAY TO A CIRCLE
> (they have a semicircular part)
>
> THINGS THAT ARE UP
>
> THINGS THAT HAVE SWIRLS
>
> THINGS THAT ARE LONG

All these rules lead to legitimate problems of definition and clarification. Such issues should not be simplified for the students, because these are exactly the ideas that can stimulate deeper thinking about classification. In particular, three issues often arise as students of this age sort:

- A category can be seen but is very difficult to describe. For example, the students whose rule was THINGS THAT ARE UP used a birthday candle and a pencil standing vertically, on their ends, to illustrate their rule. They also chose a large wooden bead and a checker. A paper clip, paper price tag, and index card did not fit their rule. Their concept seemed to be something like objects with a discernible height. They had constructed a legitimate "fuzzy" characteristic, hard to define yet real.

Continued on next page

Other students seemed to know what they meant, too; one student, attempting to guess the rule, said "they're puffy." It is very tempting to help students with such an idea by getting them to substitute a simpler rule, one that is not so hard to define (for example, leave out the bead and the checker and call the category tall and thin). Instead, help students clarify their rule simply by asking them what does and does not belong in their category and why.

■ Some descriptions require a basis for comparison. For example, the students who chose THINGS THAT ARE LONG had not really thought about what they meant by this relative term. When they began to field other students' guesses, they found they could not really agree on which objects did and did not fit their rule. Although the situation is different, the teacher's role is very similar to that described above: that is, ask students, before they challenge the rest of the class, to decide which objects fit their rule, which objects don't fit, and why. Challenge their choices and help them verbalize their reasons.

Students at this age need a great deal of experience with the comparison implicit in measurement terms like *long, heavy, big, far, tall,* or *warm.* What dimension is being considered? What is being compared to what? Even a measurement that seems exact may require further definition. One small group made their own collection of THINGS THAT ARE 2" LONG. When they found that hardly anything was exactly that length, they decided that anything between 1½ and 2½ inches was close enough.

■ Different words can describe the same characteristic. The group whose rule was THINGS THAT HAVE SWIRLS did not accept student guesses of "things that are kind of like stairs," "things that are down and up," or "things that are zigzag." There was protest when they announced their rule because other students felt they had already identified the category in different words. The teacher helped both the guessers and the rule makers explore whether their definitions were really different. In this case, the rule makers presented a good case that while zigzags and stairs had corners, swirls (like on a birthday candle and a screw) were curvy. In such a case, the teacher must, on the one hand, encourage the clarification of real differences in definition and, on the other hand, discourage students from being too rigid about guesses. If other students have guessed the concept and have accurately described the characteristics of the category, the exact word should not be at issue.

D■I■A■L■O■G■U■E■□■B■O■X

Paying Attention to the Evidence

During the activity, Guess My Rule: Thing Collections (p. 40) students try to figure out the teacher's mystery rule (THINGS THAT HAVE A POINT). Students have already guessed that a pencil, a jack, a paper clip, a screw and a plastic stirrer do fit the rule and that all other objects in the collection do not fit.

Graham [*waving his hand wildly*]: I know! I know!

What do you think, Graham?

Graham: It's THINGS THAT ARE METAL.

Why do you think that?

Graham: What?

How can you make us believe that the rule is THINGS THAT ARE METAL?

Graham: Well, the jack and the paper clip—

Helena: It can't be THINGS THAT ARE METAL because—

Wait, Helena, because I want to hear Graham's thinking about this. How were you thinking about it?

Graham: Well, I was thinking the screw and the paper clip were metal . . . [*stops, looks uncomfortable*]

Uh-huh. And do you want to think more about your idea?

Graham: Well, the pencil isn't metal, so I guess it can't be METAL THINGS.

Good thinking. Does anyone else see something to make you think THINGS THAT ARE METAL can't be the rule?

Helena: And the plastic stick isn't metal.

OK. My rule wasn't METAL. Any more ideas? This is a hard one. Tell me even if you had a good idea that you decided wasn't the rule. Did anyone have an idea you decided didn't work?

Phoebe: Well, I was thinking LONG THINGS until someone guessed the jack, and that's not long.

So you really used that clue. If I take the jack away, can anyone see a good reason why LONG THINGS still isn't the rule?

Bjorn: Yes, the craft stick isn't in the circle, and that's long.

OK, so Bjorn thought about the things that don't fit my rule. Remember, that's important to do. Who else is thinking about a rule that might work?

Olga: It's like, DIFFERENT SHAPES.

Tell us how you're thinking that DIFFERENT SHAPES works.

Olga: Well, like, the paper clip is like that [*shows the shape in the air*] and the jack is like a star.

And what did you think about the screw?

Olga: It's long.

And did they all go together somehow?

Olga: Yes, they're like, SHAPES.

Linda?

Linda: Well, it can't be SHAPES because the bead and the checker and the craft stick are all shapes and they don't fit.

Linda thinks that DIFFERENT SHAPES doesn't work because there are some shapes that don't fit my rule. Any other ideas?

Ebony: Not exactly long, but kind of long and pointy.

How would LONG AND POINTY THINGS work as the rule for the objects in the circle?

Continued on next page

continued

In this discussion, the teacher begins to require
that students give good reasons for their ideas,
rather than make unsubstantiated guesses. She
has noticed that Graham tends to guess quickly
and impulsively, considering only one or two of the
objects. She is sure he can make a more reasoned
guess if challenged to do so. Olga, on the other
hand, seems genuinely confused about how to
make a general statement about the objects. Her
overly inclusive category of SHAPES is a common
approach used by primary grade students who are
still developing an understanding of classification.
Linda's comment may help clarify why SHAPES
does not work, but Olga may not be ready to take
in this explanation. She needs continued experience in classification activities. The teacher questions students not only when she thinks they are
"wrong"; rather, she asks them to explain their
thinking as often as possible. This enables the
teacher to communicate her interest in how they
are thinking, not just in getting the correct
answer.

Sink and Float

Materials

- Thing Collections
  (1 per group)
- Tubs or basins
  (1 per group)
- Large sheets of paper
  (1 per group)
- Sheets of newspaper
  (optional)
- Student Sheet 6 (1 per
  student, homework)

What Happens

Students collect data about whether objects in their Thing Collections sink or float when placed in water. In small groups they organize the experiment, collect and record the data, organize the data, and then make a representation of their organization. Based on their findings, students pose hypotheses about the properties of objects that sink and objects that float. Their work focuses on:

- constructing their own categories to describe data they have collected
- conducting an experiment as a way of collecting and recording data
- inventing representations of data
- making hypotheses about things that sink and things that float based on the data collected

Start-Up

Today's Number Sometime during the school day, students brainstorm ways to express Today's Number. Suggest that they use both addition and subtraction in each number sentence they write. For example, if the number they are working on is 70, possible solutions include, 35 + 40 − 5 or 90 − 30 + 10. Add a card to the class counting strip and fill in the next number on the blank 200 chart. See p. 86 for a complete description of this routine.

Activity

What Sinks? What Floats?

Each group of 2–3 students will need a Thing Collection, a basin of water, and paper for recording.

Today you're going to collect data about the Thing Collections by doing an experiment. Your job is to find out which things sink and which things float. Find out as much as you can about each thing. Does it always sink? Does it always float? Does anything else happen to it? You will be recording what you find out.

If students are not used to water activities, you may want to establish some guidelines, such as no splashing. However, since this activity is usually quite absorbing for students of this age, some water is bound to get on the surrounding surfaces. You may want to spread newspapers on the floor under the tubs.

While students are conducting the sink-and-float experiment, they will need to keep track of what happens to each object. Ask students to test the objects carefully, one at a time, and write what they find out on the recording sheet. Their notes can be rough—for example, S or F for sink or float—but should include as much information as possible.

As you observe students working, encourage them to move beyond the simple categories of sink and float as they observe the objects. For example, sometimes students notice that certain objects (such as an index card) float for a while and then sink; others (such as a paper cup) sometimes float and sometimes sink, depending on how they are placed in the water. Some objects may get soggy or disintegrate when left in the water. Many students will notice other characteristics as well.

Teacher Checkpoint

Graphing Our Data

Teacher checkpoints are places for you to stop and observe students and their work. This checkpoint is an opportunity to look carefully at how students are representing data.

To begin, tell students the following:

When scientists do an experiment, they need to tell other people what they found out. Often they use graphs and pictures to show what happened.

You are going to draw pictures or graphs to show what you found out about your Thing Collection. Most of you found out which things float and which sink, and some of you found out other things too. Use your list to help you remember what was interesting and important about the objects in your collection.

Provide each group with a large sheet of paper and ask them to think about how they want to show their data. As in the earlier investigation, Sorting People and Yekttis, encourage students to use more than one way of showing what they discovered. Different students in the same group can make different representations of their findings. Emphasize the value of looking at the data in more than one way. See the **Teacher Note,** Representing Sink-and-Float Data (p. 54), for examples of student work.

If students have ideas that lead beyond the original two categories of sink and float, encourage them to create and name additional categories for their graphs or pictures. This process of deciding what categories are needed to convey the best information about the data is one of the key ideas in this unit. See the **Teacher Note,** Constructing Your Own Categories (p. 55), for an explanation of how having unlimited categorization promotes enthusiasm among students.

Class Discussion: Why Things Sink and Float

A discussion focusing on why some things sink and others float is a good way to bring this investigation to an end. Students have probably begun talking about their theories during group work. The object of this discussion is not for students to grasp the reasons for objects' sinking and floating, but rather to develop and test their own ideas by referring to the evidence they have collected. As in their work with Guess My Rule, they will need to pay attention to both positive and negative evidence. For example, if one theory is that heavier things sink, then this theory can be tested through positive examples (Do heavy things sink?) and through negative ones (Do light things not sink?). See the **Dialogue Box,** Second Graders' Theories About Sinking and Floating (p. 57), for excerpts from the discussion in one classroom.

Publishing Our Results

After the class discussion, ask each student to write a few sentences describing the results of his or her sink-and-float experiments. Or, as part of your language experience work, meet with each small group and ask them to dictate to you what was most interesting about their work.

❖ **Tip for the Linguistically Diverse Classroom** Students with limited English proficiency can draw pictures to show their results.

This investigation gives students an opportunity to publish the results of their data collection and analysis. Publishing is one of the phases in the data analysis process, just as in the writing process. See the **Teacher Note,** Phases of Data Analysis: Learning from the Process (p. 56), for an explanation of the publishing phase as well as the other phases involved in the process of data analysis. For students at this level, it is usually not particularly useful to have each group show its graphs and report to the rest of the class. Students' oral reports rarely reflect the quality of the thinking that has gone into their work, and it is hard for the class to be attentive through a series of seven or eight similar reports. However, it can be very effective to publish students' writing and their representations as an attractive bulletin board display or as a book for the class library.

Weekly Log This is a good time for students to record in their Weekly Logs the work that they have done in collecting data. Encourage them to share any problems they are having and any interesting information they found.

Sessions 3 and 4 Follow-Up

Playing Guess My Rule with Thing Collections Students play Guess My Rule with someone at home using the Thing Collections they assembled previously. Students play several times and represent how the Thing Collections was sorted for two of the games on Student Sheet 6. Remind students to refer to Student Sheet 5 for game rules. Have extra copies available for students who may need them.

 **Homework**

More Science Experiments A task for another sink-and-float session comes from Delta Education, Elementary Science Study unit on sinking and floating. Take one thing that floats and find a way to make it sink; then take one thing that sinks and find a way to make it float.

 **Extension**

What other properties of the Thing Collection can be discovered through experimentation, observation, and recording? You may have some ideas that fit with your science curriculum, and students can also brainstorm their own ideas for experimentation. A sequence similar to the one suggested for these sessions on sinking and floating can be followed to explore such questions as: Which are heavy and which are light? Which things are pulled by a magnet? Which things conduct electricity?

Note: The development of this investigation was influenced by an Elementary Science Study unit, Sink or Float, which the authors used in their own classrooms. For further work in this area, use the unit itself, which is available from Delta Education, Inc., P.O. Box 915, Hudson, NH 03051. A related unit, Clay Boats, is also available from Delta.

Teacher Note

Representing Sink-and-Float Data

Shown on this page are some of the ways second and third graders have represented their findings from the sink-and-float experiment. While they vary considerably, all show the data clearly and effectively.

FLOAt	BOTH	SugNC
1. CUP	RUBBR BAND	1. PAPER
2. PAINT BRUSH	JACK	2. CLAY
3. STRA		3. PAPER CLIP
4. STRiNG		
5. PLASTiC RiNG		
6. SPONg		
7. CANDLE		
8. LiD		
9. TOTHPiCK		

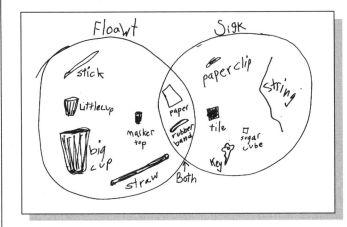

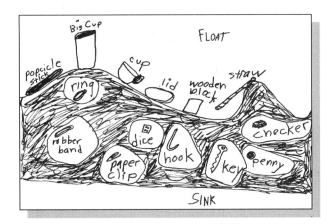

Constructing Your Own Categories

One key element in picturing categorical data is deciding on the categories themselves. Too often, data collection and representation in the primary classroom are tied to predetermined categories. That is, the categories are defined before the data are collected. In one classroom, for example, some students decided to do a survey about favorite foods. Anticipating the difficulties students would have in organizing the wide variety of answers they were likely to get, the teacher suggested that they limit their survey to five predetermined choices. The students chose five foods—pizza, ice cream, peanut butter, potato chips, and spaghetti. While this step certainly simplified their task, it also obscured the richness and diversity they might have seen in their results. Unfortunately, the students also lost some of their initial enthusiasm at this point in the process; this more limited survey was much less interesting to them than their original idea.

The sink-and-float experiment demonstrates that important categories may not be known ahead of time, before data collection and analysis. As students experiment and learn more about their data, some realize that sink and float alone do not adequately describe all the phenomena they are encountering. Here is part of a discussion in one small group:

Salim: The paper crumpled up and it broke into little pieces.

Jeffrey: The paper drowned.

Jess: The screw drowned and the pipe cleaner sinks.

Jeffrey: But the plastic stick is halfway, the stick part goes down and the top stays up.

Salim: But it never goes all the way down; it's not like the screw.

Jess: And the paper cup, it sinks and floats and gets softer.

[*The teacher, circulating and observing the class, overhears the last remark.*]

How could it sink *and* float?

Jess: First it floats, then it sinks when the water goes in, and it sinks and gets softer.

Salim: But you can make it just float if you put it down so the water doesn't go in.

Jeffrey: If things sink, we're going to put a column with S, and one with F for floats.

Salim: And we need one for sink and float, S and F.

Jess: But don't count the things that float and get soft and sink. If it gets soft and sinks, we need a whole new column for that.

This group actually ended up with five columns: (1) sink, (2) float, (3) sink and float, (4) floated, got soft, sank, and (5) sank, got soft. Other groups invented their own versions of these and other categories: sinks quickly; sinks slowly; sinks then floats; sometimes sinks, sometimes floats; floats if put down softly.

Only through observing, recording, and thinking about the data can students construct truly meaningful categories that provide important information about their results. This process encourages even young children to begin to make their own observations and draw their own conclusions. They encounter an important idea about data analysis—that different observers may see the data in different ways, and that each observer has the chance to contribute a new and interesting idea through a different way of seeing and describing.

Phases of Data Analysis: Learning from the Process

The process of data analysis is similar to many other creative processes. Students doing data analysis follow the same processes that adults do; the analyses may be less complex, but the procedures are the same. The teacher's role is relatively subtle—shaping the process, asking questions that guide students' progress toward their goals, listening and responding to their ideas and theories. Students have original and interesting things to say, and the teacher provides an environment that enriches and supports students' self-expression.

Data analysis has many similarities to the process approach to writing, which typically includes four phases. The process starts with a planning phase (often called prewriting or brainstorming). Next is the writing phase, when a very rough draft of ideas is put down on paper. The third phase is revision or rewriting, when the writer elaborates, clarifies, restructures, and edits the piece. The final phase is publication, when the writer's completed piece is shared with others. These processes may be reiterated until the piece of writing is finished.

Data analysis has four phases parallel to those in the writing process.

Phase One: Brainstorming and planning. Students discuss, debate, and think about their research question. In some cases, defining and agreeing on the question may take a considerable amount of time. Having defined the question and agreed on terms, students consider possible sources of data, ways of recording them, and how they might organize themselves to collect needed information.

Phase Two: Putting it on paper. For the collection and representation of data, students might make lists or "sketch graphs" as first drafts of the information on which they base their developing theories. Students represent the data in a variety of ways to help them describe the important features. They use their first drafts as tools as they look for relationships and patterns in the data.

Phase Three: Revising. Writers are encouraged to share their drafts with their peers in order to determine how an audience perceives their work. Similarly, in the data analysis process, students often present their sketch graphs, preliminary findings, and beginning theories to their working group in order to see whether their interpretations seem supported by the data and whether others see things they haven't noticed. Revision in data analysis may include finding new ways to organize and represent the data, developing better descriptions of the data, collecting additional data, or refining the research questions and collecting a different kind of data.

Phase Four: Publishing. The nature of "publishing" the results of data analysis varies, just as it does for a story or essay. Sometimes students develop theories that are the basis for a report on a particular topic; at other times they develop theories that inspire further investigation. A complete report of a data analysis investigation may involve a written description of the study with conclusions and recommendations, final presentation graphs of information previously displayed in working graphs, or a verbal or written presentation of the report to an interested audience.

When teachers think about the writing process, their roles as facilitators and helpers seem familiar and obvious. Of course students need time to think and revise their work! Of course they need to be challenged and led, sensitively, to the next level of awareness. The writing process seems more familiar to most of us than the mathematics process because we, too, have done writing.

The process of data analysis needs the same kind of teacher support. Students need to try their ideas, to rough them out, to be challenged and encouraged to go farther in their thinking. It is important that they have time to think and to consider options—and that they see their work as part of a process. There are many ways to approach a question and many conclusions to be drawn. Like writing, mathematical investigation is a creative blend of precision and imagination.

◼ D I A L O G U E ☐ B O X ◼

Second Graders' Theories About Sinking and Floating

During the discussion Why Things Sink and Float (p. 52), the teacher is asking students, "Do you have any ideas now about why some things sink and some things float? Did anything surprise you? Did some things you thought would sink float and some things you thought would float sink?"

Paul: Anything with an air pocket or plastic or foam will float.

Phoebe: The screw sinks because it was heavy; it was made out of metal.

So we have two ideas, one reason why some things floated and one reason why some things sank.

Laura: Because heavy stuff sinks and light stuff floats.

What does she mean by heavy?

Harris: It sinks to the ground, heavy.

Olga: You can feel it.

Jeffrey: I don't agree about heavy things sinking.

Why not, Jeffrey?

Jeffrey: Not all stuff that's heavy sinks because the plastic box, we put that in, and it didn't sink.

Karina: Yes, and we even put things in it. We put in the screw, and it still didn't sink!

Does anyone else have an idea about this? Do light things float and heavy things sink?

Graham: I don't sink. I can float on the water and stay up.

Ebony: Once I was in a big pond and I picked up a rock and it made me sink.

Can you think of anything else heavy, not something in the classroom, that floats?

Tim: A boat.

Temara: A boat can sink or float.

A boat sinks?

Temara: If there's a hole in it, there's a shipwreck.

Angel: The water goes into it and pushes it down.

So the water can push it down? Hmm. So what are you all thinking now about whether heavy things sink and light things float?

Simon: It doesn't matter how heavy or light it is.

Jeffrey: Because a heavy thing might be able to swim or lay on the water.

And are there any light things that sank when you tried them?

Ayaz: Yes, the paper clip sank.

Jess: And the index card. The water went over it and pushed it down.

Any other ideas about why some of the things you tried sank and why some things floated?

Salim: Because of the water skin.

The water skin?

Salim: Like the plastic stick, the stirrer. Sometimes it floated if you put it down real carefully because the water skin holds it up, and if you push it under the water, it will just sink.

So sometimes something floated because the water skin held it up? Who had another thing that floated and can give us a reason—the same one as Salim's or a different one—why you think it floated?

Juanita: The plastic container because of the air. If it has air in it, it floats. But if it doesn't have air in it, it can't float.

Ayaz: And the foam ball. It has more air in it than the screw or the paper clip, so it floats.

That is like what Paul said at the beginning about an air pocket. Are there other things you can think of that have air in them?

INVESTIGATION 3

Animals in the Neighborhood

A Note on Investigations 3 and 4

Investigations 3 and 4 offer two final projects for this unit. You may do both, or you might select the one that best fits your situation and the interests of your students.

The first project, Animals in the Neighborhood, provides further experience in developing categories and sorting data. After organizing the data based on how animals move, students devise their own data question about animals in the neighborhood, sort the data, and create a presentation graph.

In the second project, Scary Things, students collect data about what they are afraid of and compare this information to data they collect from adults about their fears when they were children. The Scary Things investigation has been used successfully by teachers in a variety of schools in urban, suburban, and rural settings. Second-grade students are engaged by the topic, can draw on their own experiences, and are eager to collect data from others. Because students collect data from their family members, it also provides connections between home and school.

A discussion of scary things may tap into students' deepest feelings and concerns. All students should be able to participate freely, and none of their ideas should be rejected as inappropriate. If you prefer not to undertake this topic, use Animals in the Neighborhood (Sessions 1–3) as the final data analysis project.

What Happens

Session 1: How Animals Move   Students brainstorm a list of animals living in the neighborhood. In small groups they categorize the animals according to how they move (fly, swim, walk, hop, and so on) and construct group graphs showing the neighborhood animals in those categories.

Sessions 2 and 3: Representing Data in More than One Way   Using the data they collected in the previous session, small groups devise a new question about neighborhood animals. They sort the animals into categories to answer this question and create a presentation graph to show how they have sorted their data.

Mathematical Emphasis

- Constructing categories to describe data
- Articulating clear definitions of categories
- Organizing categorical data

What to Plan Ahead of Time

Materials

- Stick-on notes or index cards: about 200 (Session 1)
- Chart paper (Sessions 1–3)
- Large sheets of paper: about 20–30 sheets (Sessions 1–3)
- Crayons or markers (Sessions 2–3)

Other Preparation

- Duplicate student sheets and teaching resources (located at the end of this unit) in the following quantities. If you have Student Activity Booklets, no copying is needed.

For Session 1

Student Sheet 7, Animals in the Neighborhood (p. 144): 1 per group of 3–4 students

Student Sheet 8, Animals Near My Home (p. 145): 1 per student (homework)

For Session 2–3

Student Sheet 7, Animals in the Neighborhood (p. 144): 1 per student

How Animals Move

Materials

- Chart paper
- Stick-on notes or index cards (about 20–30 per group of 3–4 students)
- Large sheets of paper (1 per group)
- Student Sheet 7 (1 per group)
- Student Sheet 8 (1 per student, homework)

What Happens

Students brainstorm a list of animals living in the neighborhood. In small groups they categorize the animals according to how they move (fly, swim, walk, hop, and so on) and construct group graphs showing the neighborhood animals in those categories. Their work focuses on:

- constructing categories to organize data
- representing data

Start-Up

Today's Number   Sometime during the school day, students brainstorm ways to express Today's Number using pennies, nickels, dimes, or quarters. For example, if Today's Number is 72, possible solutions include: 25¢ + 25¢ + 10¢ + 10¢ + 1¢ + 1¢ or 25¢ + 10¢ + 10¢ + 10¢ + 10¢ + 5¢ + 1¢ + 1¢. Add a number card to the counting strip and fill in the next number on the blank 200 chart. For a complete description of this routine, see p. 86.

Activity

Naming Animals That Live in Our Neighborhood

Remind students that they have been working on ways of collecting and sorting information.

Today we'll be collecting data by thinking about what we already know about the animals that live in our neighborhood.

Suppose you went on a walk near your home or around the school. It could be today or it could be some other time of year. What animals have you ever seen that live in the neighborhood? Some animals are easy to see and some are hard to see. Close your eyes and try to picture different places you have walked near your home or the school and what animals you've seen in these places.

Encourage students to think carefully about animals seen during different seasons of the year and those that might be difficult to find or hard to see (such as spiders). After some thinking time, invite students to name the animals they have thought of. List the animals on chart paper or on the chalkboard. Students can decide whether they want to include pets or just animals found in their natural habitats.

There may be some animals students have seen whose names they don't know. Find some way to identify them—maybe other students know what they are, or make up a name for them (silver bathtub bug, little yellow bird).

A long list may emerge in 10 minutes of brainstorming. The **Teacher Note,** Animals in the Neighborhood (p. 63), provides one urban second grade classroom's list of animals. Keep your list posted for the next activity.

❖   **Tip for the Linguistically Diverse Classroom**   Draw pictures of the animals on the list, or find and cut out pictures in magazines. Glue the pictures next to each animal name on the list.

Sorting Animals by How They Move

The following discussion can be brief since small groups will be exploring the activity question.

Do you remember how you made categories to show what happened during your sink-and-float experiments? When scientists study animals, they sort them into groups to help them think about how different animals are alike and how they're different. Today we're going to think about our neighborhood animals and create categories for how they move. Who can tell me something about how one of these animals moves around?

Write on the board the words that come up in this discussion; for example, *walks, flies, crawls, swims, hops.*

In your groups, you are going to sort the animals on our list into categories to show how they move. You can use some of our movement words, but you don't have to use all of them. You might think of your own categories that are different from these. Your group will decide together on your categories.

Provide each group with enough index cards or stick-on notes so each animal can be written on a different card and a large sheet of paper. You may need to provide some suggestions for ways to divide up this task.

To sort the animals, your group will need to copy each animal name from our list onto a card. Put one name on each card. If your group divides up the work and each person copies a few animals, it won't take too long to copy the names. Once you have copied the data and you have checked to see that you have all the animals on the chart, you can start putting the animals together and naming the categories for how they move. When everyone agrees on how to group the animals, you can record your data on Student Sheet 7, Animals in the Neighborhood.

❖ **Tip for the Linguistically Diverse Classroom** As students with limited English proficiency copy the animal names on cards, encourage them to draw a picture next to each animal's name.

Observing the Students Circulate around the classroom and encourage students to arrange and rearrange their animals into groups. Some students will prefer to find animals that go together first and to decide what to name the categories after they have grouped their animals. Other students may start out with certain categories in mind. Help these students to be flexible in finding new categories and in modifying or changing their old categories if some animals do not fit their initial scheme.

Encourage students to sort the animals in whatever ways make sense to them and to articulate why they are putting certain animals into certain categories. It's important that students discuss their reasoning with one another. Students may not always agree, but they should be encouraged to resolve differences by clarifying the definitions of their categories. See the **Dialogue Box,** Does a Spider Walk? (p. 64), for examples of how a teacher assisted students in clarifying their definitions.

As students make their decisions, they group the stick-on notes in bar graphs, clusters, or whatever arrangement they think of. The **Teacher Note,** Animals in the Neighborhood (p. 63), shows samples of second graders' categorization. These graphs need not be permanent. If students are using stick-on notes, they can move the notes to a large piece of newsprint when they are satisfied with their arrangement. Since students will be reusing these data in the next two sessions, they should not glue or tape the data to the paper.

Note: Students will begin the next session by discussing their representations of the data. Suggest that students carefully stack their graphs on a bookshelf or out-of-the-way spot until the next math session.

Session 1 Follow-Up

🏠 **Homework**

Animals Near My Home Students look for animals in, around, or near their home. They record what they found on Student Sheet 8, Animals Near My Home.

Animals in the Neighborhood

Let students experiment with different arrangements for their categories. Here is a partial list of animals (including pets) generated by a second grade class in an urban school:

dog	raccoon
cardinal	blue jay
mosquito	spider
butterfly	rabbit
mouse	grasshopper
turtle	crow
cat	ladybug
fly	squirrel
little bird	frog
bee	cockroach
rat	ant
worm	pigeon

The students set up a variety of categories and arrangements such as the ones shown here.

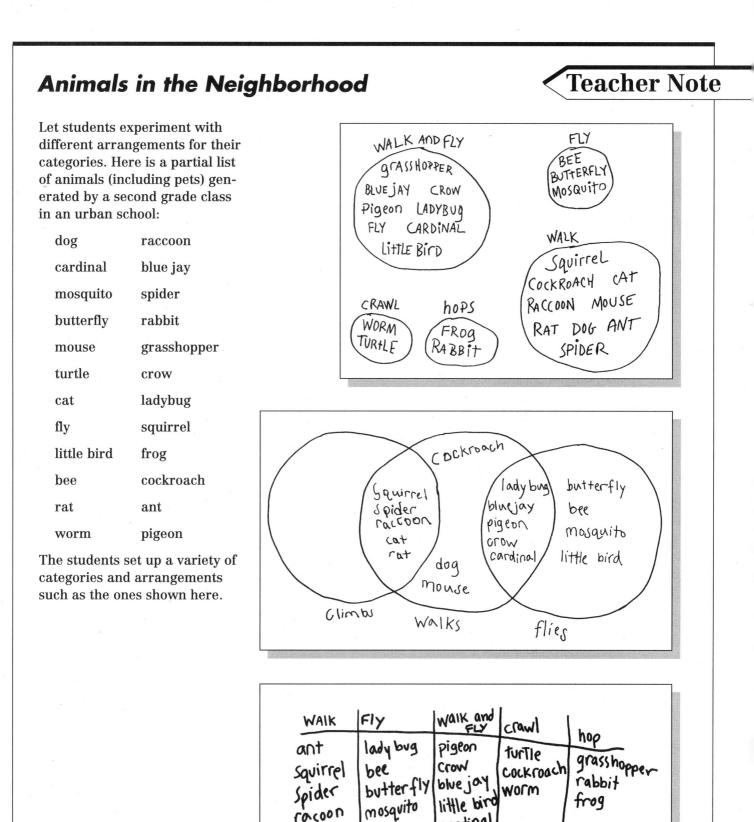

═ DIALOGUE BOX ═

Does a Spider Walk?

In a discussion during the activity Sorting Animals by How They Move (p. 61), students talk about ways to group the animals on the class list.

Salim: I've got one for FLIES.

Franco: What are you going to put in it?

Salim: Grasshopper.

Franco: It doesn't fly, though.

Laura: It doesn't crawl and it doesn't walk.

Franco: It can walk.

Olga: It hops.

Franco: No, it jumps.

Salim: Yes, jumps.

Franco: Put jump. Let's make a card for JUMPS.

Olga: And rabbit goes in JUMPS, too, and frog.

Laura: What about spider?

Franco: It walks. It has legs.

Salim: No, walk isn't right. It's not like a dog or something. It can go up the walls and upside down on the ceiling. It climbs.

Olga: Let's make one for CLIMBS.

Salim: Then I think raccoon goes there, too. It climbs up trees.

Laura: [*Starts to move other cards into* CLIMBS] Squirrels can go up trees, and cats can, too.

Franco: But you're taking everything out of WALKS. This is too hard. I don't think we should put CLIMBS.

[*The teacher steps in, overhearing the last exchange.*]

You don't think you should use CLIMBS?

Franco: No, Laura's taking everything out of WALKS.

Laura: I am not.

What started you thinking about CLIMBS as a category?

Salim: The spider, because it can go on the ceiling.

Uh-huh. So that wasn't the same as an animal that walks?

Salim: Yes, cause, like, I walk, but I can't go upside down.

And what did you think, Franco?

Franco: Well, then Laura was going to put squirrel and cat and everything, but a cat doesn't climb all the time.

So you think a spider and a cat are really different in the way they get around?

Franco: Yes.

What do the rest of you think about that? Are a spider and a cat the same or different?

Olga: Well, I guess they're different. I mean they kind of both walk, but a spider sticks on with its feet.

Can anything else you have here do that?

Laura: Well, a fly can. It can crawl around anywhere.

Salim: Yes, and a cockroach.

Franco: Yuck.

Well, it seems to me you have an important idea here. You're really thinking about the differences between things that can walk only on the floor or the ground and things that can walk anywhere.

[*The teacher moves on to another group.*]

Olga: So let's put CLIMBS, but we'll just put things that can go anywhere, so squirrels and cats stay in WALKS.

Continued on next page

DIALOGUE BOX

continued

Franco: OK.

The teacher intervenes to help students articulate and clarify the ideas that are emerging. The teacher helps students think a little harder about the differences between walking and climbing, and points out that they are doing interesting thinking ("you have an important idea here"), but does not resolve the discussion for them.

Representing Data in More Than One Way

Materials

- Graphs of animal data from Session 1
- Chart paper
- Large sheets of paper (1 per group)
- Crayons or markers
- Student Sheet 7 (1 per student)

What Happens

Using the data they collected in the previous session, small groups devise a new question about neighborhood animals. They sort the animals into categories to answer this question and create a presentation graph to show how they have sorted their data. Their work focuses on:

- representing data in more than one way

Start-Up

How Many Pockets?   The routine How Many Pockets? gives students an opportunity to collect, represent, and interpret numerical data through an experience that is meaningful to them. As students collect data about pockets throughout the year, they create natural opportunities to compare quantities and to see that data can change over time.

How Many Pockets? is one of the classroom routines that occur regularly throughout the *Investigations* curriculum. The complete write-up of this routine, which includes several versions, can be found on p. 89. If you are doing the full-year grade 2 *Investigations* curriculum, students will be familiar with this routine and you should proceed with the following activity. If this is your first *Investigations* unit, familiarize yourself with this routine and do the basic pocket activity with students *instead* of the following activity.

Calculating the Total Number of Pockets   Divide students into groups of four or five. Ask each group to find the total number of pockets they are wearing. Then collect the data from each group and record them on the board. Using this information, students work in pairs to determine the total number of pockets being worn by the class. Ask students to share the strategies they used to find the total.

Allow about 10 minutes for students to briefly discuss their ideas from the previous session for organizing the data on animal movements. After students report on the categories they chose, pose one of these questions:

- Do most of the animals in our neighborhood fly? walk? crawl?
- Are there any categories in which we have no animals or very few? Why is that?

Encourage students to use their representations to back up their ideas about these questions.

Sharing Representations for How Animals Move

Introduce this activity by telling students the following:

Today you're going to work in groups again to show something about the neighborhood animals, but this time your group is going to decide what to show. Last time we sorted the animals to answer the question "How do these animals move?" But there are many other questions we could ask about these animals. Can you think of other questions?

Accept ideas from students for 5 minutes. As students offer ideas, list them on chart paper or on the chalkboard. You may need to start off the discussion with a few sample questions.

How Else Can We Sort Animals?

Questions You Can Ask About Neighborhood Animals

Where do the animals live?

What do they eat?

How big are they?

Are they fierce or gentle?

What kinds of sounds do they make?

In which seasons of the year can we find them?

Which animals are tame? Which are wild?

Organize students into small groups (you will probably want to keep the same working groups as in the previous session). Explain to students that just as they made categories when they considered the question "How do these animals move?," they will need to think about new categories based on the new question they are investigating.

Organizing the Data: Constructing New Categories Students work in their groups. They first decide what question they will ask, then use their index cards or stick-ons (from the graphs they made in the previous session) to arrange and rearrange their data as they choose categories. Note that students could look at an attribute such as size, even if they do not know exact measurements, by defining categories such as SMALL, MEDIUM, and BIG, or SMALLER THAN A MOUSE, AS BIG AS A MOUSE, and BIGGER THAN A MOUSE. Not all animals from the previous session need to be included. New animals may be added.

Collecting More Data: Using Resources During this process, questions are bound to arise. Students will find that they are not sure or that they disagree about how to classify some of the animals. Tell each group to record their unanswered questions; for example: Are raccoons fierce or gentle? Is a mouse bigger or smaller than 6 inches? What does a crow eat? Can a squirrel sometimes be a pet? Help students do their own research to find answers to these questions through one or more of the following actions:

- Take a class trip to the school or public library so that students can look at books about animals.

- Set up a library corner in the classroom with books and magazines that have information about local animals. (*Ranger Rick,* a monthly magazine for children published by the National Wildlife Federation, is one good source.)

- Invite a speaker from a local science museum, wildlife refuge, or branch of the Audubon Society to answer students' questions about local animals. Such a speaker may also be able to provide information on other animals that live in the vicinity but are not often seen.

Activity

Making a Presentation Graph

When students have developed their categories and have sorted the data, each group jointly makes a more permanent presentation graph that shows their question, their categories, and how they sorted the animals into the categories. Some groups might simply paste the stick-on notes they have been using onto large sheets of paper. Others may want to draw their graphs. Encourage students to decide on their own way of representing the data. Some may want to include pictures of the animals. Students can begin work on the graphs in Session 2 and devote all of Session 3 to finishing them.

When groups have finished their presentation graphs, distribute a copy of Student Sheet 7, Animals in the Neighborhood, to each student. Encourage students to discuss the questions about their data raised on the student sheet, but explain that each student in the group must fill out his or her own sheet. Depending on the complexity of each group's representation, you may or may not want to modify Exercise 3, in which students draw a picture of their representation. The main reason for doing this is so that you can have some record of the graph to which each student contributed.

The sharing of representations can happen in a variety of ways, depending on how much time is available. Groups might share their graphs with the class. You could pair up groups and have them present their information to each other. You might post all of the representations around the classroom and allow groups to visit each graph. Or you might have a more public presentation by inviting family members or other classes to view each representation while students explain their grouping process and their thinking.

Sessions 2 and 3 Follow-Up

 **Extension**

Collecting More Data   If possible, take a class walk around the neighborhood and record all the animals you see. This is a good opportunity for students to practice being careful observers. You might assign pairs of students to watch for particular kinds of animals; for example, some pairs might focus on ANIMALS THAT CAN BE SEEN ABOVE OUR HEADS (birds, squirrels), other pairs on ANIMALS THAT CAN BE SEEN ON THE GROUND (ants, dogs).

Grouping animals according to characteristics is an activity that could be done several times during the school year. Keep students' graphs so that you can use them to compare animal populations in different seasons. What animals do you find in the fall? winter? spring? Are there more flying animals in the spring? Are there fewer animals that walk on the ground in the winter, or are they just harder to see? How many of each type of animal do you see during a week? The collecting and recording processes could be part of a science curriculum that focuses on changing seasons, animal lives, or interdependent relationships in the environment.

Invite an adult who has lived in the area since childhood to speak to the class. What changes have there been in animal life over the years?

These activities can lead to new projects and new ways to sort the animals. Depending on the community, students may have little detailed knowledge about the animals that live in their area. One urban third grade, for example, decided to study types of spiders. They took walks to find spiders, brought spiders into the classroom (temporarily) for observation, drew pictures, wrote descriptions, and read books about spiders. For data analysis activities, they sorted spiders according to which ones live outdoors and which indoors, as well as by the types of webs they construct.

INVESTIGATION 4

Scary Things

What Happens

Session 1: What Scares Us? The class listens to a story concerning children's fears such as *There's a Nightmare in My Closet.* Students discuss what things scare them, draw pictures of their "most scary thing," and group the pictures into categories. The class develops a bar graph using their categories. For homework, students talk with their adult family members or friends about what scared them when they were children.

Sessions 2 and 3: Comparing Scary Things Data
Students organize the scary things data they collected from adults. They make a representation of these data and compare the adult data with their own class data.

Mathematical Emphasis

- Collecting and recording survey data
- Constructing categories to describe the data
- Comparing two data sets
- Experiencing the data analysis process
- Making presentation graphs and reporting on data analysis activities

What to Plan Ahead of Time

Materials

- *There's a Nightmare in My Closet* by Mercer Mayer (Session 1, optional)
- Index cards or stick-on notes: about 300 (Sessions 1–3)
- Crayons or markers (Sessions 1–3)
- Chart paper (Sessions 1–3)
- Tape or thumbtacks (Sessions 1–3)
- Half-sheets of paper: about 100–150 (Sessions 1–3)
- Large sheets of paper: about 15 (Sessions 2–3)

Other Preparation

- Duplicate student sheets and teaching resources (located at the end of this unit) in the following quantities. If you have Student Activity Booklets, no copying is needed.

  For Session 1

  Student Sheet 9, Adult Scary Things Data (p. 146): 1 per student (homework)

  For Sessions 2–3

  Student Sheet 10, Solving Problems with Imaginary Data (p. 147): 1 per student (homework)

- Read *There's a Nightmare in My Closet* to acquaint yourself with what things the boy in the story was scared of. Or read a similar book dealing with children's fears. (Session 1)

- You may choose to provide half sheets of paper rather than index cards or stick-on notes for students' drawings of scary things. (Session 1)

What Scares Us?

Materials

- *There's a Nightmare in My Closet* by Mercer Mayer (optional)
- Index cards, stick-on notes, or half sheets of paper (1 per student)
- Crayons or markers
- Chart paper
- Tape or thumbtacks
- Student Sheet 9 (1 per student, homework)

What Happens

The class listens to a story concerning children's fears such as *There's a Nightmare in My Closet*. Students discuss what things scare them, draw pictures of their "most scary thing," and group the pictures into categories. The class develops a bar graph using their categories. For homework, students talk with their adult family members or friends about what scared them when they were children. Their work focuses on:

- defining categories for data
- organizing data
- interviewing others and collecting data

Start-Up

Today's Number   Sometime during the school day, students brainstorm ways to express Today's Number using three or more numbers. For example, if Today's Number is 75, possible addends include: 25 + 25 + 25, 20 + 20 + 20 + 15, or 50 + 10 + 10 + 5. Add a number card to the counting strip and fill in the next number on the blank 200 chart.

Activity

Talking About Scary Things

We are going to collect data about things people are scared of—what children are scared of and what adults were scared of when they were children. To help you start thinking about scary things, I am going to read a book about one child's idea of what's scary.

If you have the book *There's a Nightmare in My Closet,* read it aloud to the class. If you don't have the book, you may want to retell it in your own words using the following story line:

A little boy is scared of a nightmare in his closet. One night, he decides to wait for the nightmare to come out so he can get rid of it. When the nightmare comes out, he threatens to shoot it with his toy gun. The nightmare starts to cry and the little boy comforts it. He tucks the nightmare into bed, and they both go to sleep.

Alternatively, you may want to read another book dealing with children's fears, or simply share something that scared you when you were a child.

❖ **Tip for the Linguistically Diverse Classroom** If you tell a story aloud without a visual aid, ask volunteers to act out the story to make it comprehensible for students with limited English proficiency. You can also draw sketches on the chalkboard to convey key words.

Ask students to share what sorts of things they, or others, are scared of. To make this discussion a little less personal, good discussion starters are: "What were you scared of when you were little?" "What are children your age scared of?" or "What are other people you know scared of?" By phrasing the questions this way, students do not have to admit that they're scared of anything. No matter how you phrase the question, students will be eager to share stories about themselves, their friends, or people in their family. See the **Dialogue Box,** What Are You Scared Of? (p. 77), for descriptions of things that scare typical second grade students. In this first session, allow students to recount examples and tell stories but keep the discussion moving so that it doesn't get stuck on a single topic, such as a scary movie.

Handle this discussion sensitively, since there are very real, as well as imaginary things that frighten students. See the **Teacher Note,** Starting to Talk About Scary Things (p. 76), for suggestions on how to manage this discussion.

Activity

Our Most Scary Things

Write on the chalkboard "Our Most Scary Things." Tell students that you are going to make a graph to show their ideas.

Ask students to choose something that they think is scary and draw it on an index card or stick-on note. (Or you may choose to provide half sheets of paper for these drawings.) They can pick something from the session's first discussion or something that they have thought of since. Students should also write something to describe their picture, in case you can't tell what the picture shows. Their pictures do not need to include names. Give students about 5 minutes to draw their pictures.

Collect the pictures. Use the board or chart paper to jot down all students' descriptions of their pictures. (See the sample list of descriptions from a second grade class, p. 76.) Then read the list aloud, or have students read it.

Organizing the Data: Putting Things Together Discuss with students possible ways to group the scary things on their list.

You've thought of a lot of scary things. Let's see if there are any that go together. Remember how you sorted your Thing Collection into groups of things that went together? Are there some of these scary things that could go into a group together?

Take students' suggestions for grouping things and write them on chart paper or on the chalkboard. For example, categories might include monsters, animals, scary places, the dark, mean older kids. Students will have to think about names for their categories, what fits in the categories, and how inclusive to make them. It is usually easier for students at this age to think first about which scary things go together than about what to call the category. See the **Dialogue Box,** What Goes with Haunted Houses? (p. 78) for examples of how some second graders grouped scary things.

As students come to agree on categories and which pictures fit in them, you can move the pictures into groups (using small pieces of tape or tacks) so that the students can see which pictures are classified and which are still left to sort. You will want to save this representation, so if you are posting data on the chalkboard, consider taping a sheet of chart paper or newsprint on the board and posting data on that.

Organizing the Data: Making a Graph Using students' pictures and the categories they have generated, make a graph by listing the categories across the bottom of the chart paper or chalkboard, and then taping or tacking each card above the name of its category. If there are a few unresolved issues, have students decide what to do. There may be one or two pictures that do not fall easily into any category and end up alone. Display the graph in a place where it can be seen easily during the rest of the Scary Things sessions.

Session 1 Follow-Up

Adult Scary Things Data   Ask students the following questions "What do you think you'd find out if you asked adult family members or friends what they used to be scared of? When they were your age, do you think they were scared of the same things you are now?" After some discussion, tell students that they will be carrying out their own survey to find out what adults were scared of when they were younger. Agree on exactly what question to ask and write it on the chalkboard. For example, "What scared you the most when you were younger?" Students can ask any adults they know—parents, grandparents, and neighbors. One way to organize this survey is to make every child responsible for asking the survey question to two adults for homework.

Homework

Distribute Student Sheet 9, Adult Scary Things Data, to give students an organized way to record their findings. Students can copy the survey question onto the top section of the sheet.

Some students may be interested in collecting more data about scary things from students their own age. After school, each student could ask one or two other children who are in other classes. Or you could arrange for some of your students to take a survey in another classroom. Add the new data to the bar graph. The new data may prompt students to change or add to their categories.

Note: The data students collect will be used in the next session.

Students will have a lot to say about this topic. The discussion is likely to wander in many different directions. Students will want to tell stories about their own scary experiences. Teachers have found that it is a good idea to let this discussion range widely and not to worry about focusing it during this first session.

Inevitably, students' real fears and concerns will emerge in this discussion. Teachers have used this investigation to provide support for students who have real fears; students find it reassuring to hear that they are not the only ones who are scared of something. Some teachers have been willing to volunteer information about their own fears. Even if a student does not verbalize a particular fear he or she has, simply having this topic allowed and encouraged in the classroom can help students overcome the isolation they can feel when they think that fears must be kept hidden and secret.

Manage the discussion so that it does not get stuck on one topic. For example, in one classroom, students talked a great deal about one or two particular horror videos. Eventually, in order to elicit some new ideas, the teacher needed to

say, "It certainly sounds as if a lot of you are scared by these videos. Now, what about some very different kinds of things that can be scary?"

What might be considered difficult topics can arise in this discussion. Often a simple, matter-of-fact response can acknowledge and include a child's suggestion without raising complex issues that the group as a whole might not be ready for. For example, in one class a student suggested "gangs in my neighborhood." Over the next few days the teacher followed up with discussions about peer pressure and feeling safe at school and at home.

It is critical to accept as legitimate all the fears students raise. Comments such as, "Oh, you don't need to be afraid of that, that's just make-believe," or "Of course, you know there's really nothing under your bed," appear to define some children's fears as less legitimate than others. Almost all of us have had a scary experience that seems silly in retrospect, but there's no denying that we certainly felt scared at the time. Acknowledge and accept students' stories matter-of-factly, communicating the idea that we're all afraid of things sometimes.

Some Second Graders' Scary Things

nightmares	drowning	being chased by a person with a cat
the dark	monsters with big eyes	an imaginary roach on my mirror
alleys that are messed up	my cousin	my brother jumping out at me
drunk people	matches	a boat in a thunderstorm
snakes	being robbed	my brother fell out of his crib
getting killed	loud-barking dogs	my first time at home alone
wolves	bats	getting into a fight
mice and rats	strangers	vampires
being alone	murderers	scary movies
wild cats	haunted houses	war

DIALOGUE BOX

What Are You Scared Of?

The teacher has read the book *There's a Nightmare in My Closet* to the class, and the students identified things that scared the boy in the story. In this discussion during the activity Talking About Scary Things (p. 72), students are now describing things that scare them.

Now that we've talked about the book we read this morning, let's talk about the kinds of things that you think are scary. You can either tell us what scares you or what things scare people you know.

Karina: When I watch a scary movie, when it's over I have a dream of it.

Movies sometimes scare you.

Camilla: Sometimes after I watch something with scary things, when I go to sleep, I dream about them and I make them worse.

Ayaz: One day I went to bed and I heard this noise but I found out it was my mother in the kitchen.

Simon: Since I don't get tired, I stay up late. I hear noises and then cars go by with their lights on. I think there are robbers in the house. Then I have a dream that they will come in and take my sister.

I know what you mean. When I was in first grade, when my sister and I were alone, we'd hear the house creak. We'd walk around with a flashlight and a hammer in case a monster might get us.

[Laughter]

Paul: Wind in the night.

Linda: Sometimes the curtains blow in and that scares me.

Helena: Sometimes I get really scared when someone comes in the room, and I'm reading and I don't hear them.

Bjorn: Yes, once my father was watching TV and I came in and touched him, and he jumped.

Because he was concentrating so hard?

Temara: Sometimes when we eat dinner, the shutters bang in the kitchen and scare me.

Jeffrey: Sometimes after a movie, I'm afraid to go to sleep because I might have nightmares.

So far, you've talked about movies, nightmares, scary noises, and being startled. A lot of you talked about things that happen at night or bedtime. Those are all things that are definitely scary! Now, can anyone think of some really different kinds of things that scare you or other people you know? It doesn't have to be just at night or bedtime.

Lila: My dad's afraid of dogs, that's why we can't have a dog. My mom told me that when he was little he got chased by a dog and had to climb up a tree, and he was really scared, so then he got scared of dogs.

That's interesting. I wonder if there are other people who are scared of some kind of animal.

Ayaz: Well, when I was little, I used to be afraid of bees.

What Goes with Haunted Houses?

The class has drawn pictures of things that scare them. In this discussion during the activity Our Most Scary Things (p. 73), students are deciding on which scary things go together and the category they fit in.

Franco: I think mine about going into the basement and Angel's about going into the shed go together.

Why do you think those two go together?

Franco: Because they're both dark.

Angel: Yes, and because they have spiderwebs.

Ayaz: And there are lots of places things could hide.

Is there anything else that could go with Angel and Franco's ideas?

Helena: Yes, going into the back of my uncle's store at night.

OK, what should we call this category?

Trini: DARK PLACES.

Is DARK PLACES OK?

Bjorn: The one about walking through an alley at night is about dark places, too.

So should walking through an alley be in this category, or is it something different? What do you think?

Ebony: I think it's different, because the cellar and the shed are inside places, and the alley is outside.

So should one category be DARK INSIDE PLACES?

[*Later*]

Olga: Put STRANGERS with MURDERERS.

[*Murmurs of protest are heard from other students.*]

What do you think about that?

Camilla: No, strangers don't have to be murderers. They could be really nice people, but you don't know that or maybe you see them coming at night so you think they're scary.

Paul: Put STRANGERS with HAUNTED HOUSES.

Why?

Paul: If you don't know someone in a haunted house, it's a stranger.

OK. Someone else?

Phoebe: I think STRANGERS go with DARK PLACES because it's like you don't know what's there in the dark and you don't know who the stranger is. That's why you're scared.

This is a hard one. There are a lot of different ideas about this. Let's think about STRANGERS some more and come back to it later. Maybe getting more categories will help us decide where to put it, or maybe we'll decide it should be all by itself.

Even though you may have clear ideas about how to categorize the scary things, try not to impose your categories on students. It is important that they struggle on their own with what goes together and what to call the categories. For example, one class included ghosts, skeletons, rats, demons, goblins, bats, maggots, and Dracula in a category they called HAUNTED HOUSES—probably not the way adults would classify these diverse scary things! Some things may fit in two categories or be hard to categorize. These are common and legitimate problems in classification. Remember that there are no absolute answers to these problems. What's important is that students think about the similarities and differences among the scary things and try to give good reasons for their ideas.

Comparing Scary Things Data

What Happens

Students organize the scary things data they collected from adults. They make a representation of these data and compare the adult data with their own class data. Their work focuses on:

- representing data
- comparing two sets of data

Start-Up

Today's Number   Sometime during the school day, students brainstorm ways to express Today's Number using doubles. For example, if Today's Number is 76, possible combinations include: 30 + 30 + 5 + 5 + 5 + 1 or 35 + 35 + 5 + 1. If you are keeping track of the number of school days, add a card to the class counting strip and fill in the next number on the blank 200 chart.

Materials

- Scary things data from adults, collected for homework
- Graph of scary things from Session 1
- Chart paper
- Index cards or stick-on notes (about 20 per group)
- Half sheets of paper for graph labels (about 10 per group)
- Large sheets of paper (1 per group)
- Crayons or markers
- Tape or thumbtacks
- Student Sheet 10 (1 per student, homework)

Because students will probably be eager to share their data on what scared adults, begin with a brief general discussion of the data they collected for homework.

What did you find out? Did you find some scary things that were the same as the things on our bar graph? Did you find some things that were different?

Write all the scary things students collected from adults on chart paper or on the chalkboard to form a class list. Then draw students' attention to the bar graph made in the previous session of their own scary things.

When we put our scary things on the graph, we figured out how we could put them together in groups so we could describe what kinds of things second graders are scared of. The categories we came up with were [*name the categories*]. Do you see any of the adults' scary things that would fit in these categories? Do you see any that don't fit? Do you think the same categories will work for the adult data?

What Scared Adults?

Allow time for students to comment on the similarities and differences between their own data and the adult data. This is a time for students to give their first impressions about the two sets of data and to start thinking about categories for the adult data. See the **Dialogue Box,** Will the Same Categories Work? (p. 85) for examples of how some second graders compared the two sets of data. There will be an opportunity to continue this discussion at the end of Session 3 when the data have been organized into pictures and graphs.

Activity

Assessment

Organizing, Classifying, and Displaying the Data

As students did previously, they will copy and then sort the data they collected from adults. Provide each group of 2–3 students with enough index cards or stick-on notes for them to copy each item from their list onto a separate card. Each group will also need a large sheet of paper.

Today you're going to figure out how to put the adult data into groups, just like you did for your own data about scary things. First you will need to copy the data from the class list onto cards. Then you'll decide on categories for the data.

Later, after you've decided on your categories, you'll make a big picture or graph of all the things that scared adults. Think hard about what goes together and what to call your categories. Just as when we did the sink-and-float experiment, different groups may come up with different ideas about what categories to use.

Students' first task is to group the adult scary things until they are satisfied with their classification. Encourage students to try various categorization plans by moving the cards around to try different groupings and to change categories, add new categories, or discard categories as needed. When they decide on a category, they can write it on a half sheet of paper in order to label that group of things.

As you move about the classroom, ask students for their reasoning—why do certain scary things fit in certain categories? Even if students' reasons don't agree with what adults might say, it's important that students discuss their reasoning with one another as much as they can, just as they did in the previous investigation, Animals in the Neighborhood.

When students feel satisfied with their categories, they can plan their graphs on the paper. Encourage them to make their representations both clear and interesting. Anyone who looks at the pictures or graphs should be able to understand clearly what they show about the data collected. Color or pictures could be used to highlight important information and attract attention to the message. The **Teacher Note,** Assessment: Looking at

Students' Data Representations (p. 84), can help you begin to assess some of the work students have done in this unit.

Post all of the final representations where the class can easily see them.

Things that scared Adults when they were children

dark places 6
monsters 3
some places 5
big and loud things 8
animals and bugs 10
all alone 3
scary people 3
getting hurt 5

Things that scared adults long ago

dark plases卌I
being left behind III
big animals卌
Scary dogs卌III

fighting卌
monsters III
falling IIII
witches III
nightmires卌卌

Comparing Scary Things of Adults and Students

Ask students to think about their own data and the adult data by asking these questions:

Which categories had many things that scare children? parents or teachers? Which categories were only for children's scary things? adults' scary things? Why might that be?

Encourage students both to make simple comparisons ("We listed scary videos and our parents didn't") and to construct theories about why these observations might be true ("Maybe they didn't have them when they were kids"). As part of this discussion, the different ways groups categorized the data will come up. Emphasize interesting differences. What did they find out about themselves? about adults? What was similar and what was different about what they said and what adults said? What surprised them? What questions do they still have about scary things data?

Students can each write a few sentences to summarize what was most interesting about their findings, or you can put together a class story about the project by having students dictate to you what should be included. These reports can be posted along with the graphs and pictures to make a final Scary Things display. If students are interested, they could present their research results to another class.

Choosing Student Work to Save

As the unit ends, you may want to use one of the following options for creating a record of students' work in this unit.

- Students look back through their folders and think about what they learned in this unit, what they remember most, and what was hard or easy for them to do. You might have students discuss these ideas with a partner or have them share ideas with the whole class, while you record their responses on chart paper.

- Depending on how you organize and collect student work, you may want to have students select some examples of their work to keep in a math portfolio. In addition, you may want to choose some examples from each student's math folder to include in the portfolio. Items such as the Guess My Rule representation, Sink-and-Float recording sheet, and representation and work from Animals in the Neighborhood and Adult Scary Things Data may be useful for assessing student growth over the school year. You may want to keep the originals and make copies of these pieces for students to take home.

- Send a selection of work home for families to see. Students can write cover letters describing their work in this unit. This work should be returned if you are keeping a year-long portfolio of mathematics work for each student.

Sessions 2 and 3 Follow-Up

Solving Problems with Imaginary Data   Students use imaginary data to figure out how many students are in an imaginary class. Then they solve a related problem that has many solutions. They record their work on Student Sheet 10.

🏠 **Homework**

Collecting More Data   One class took a new all-class survey about things that scare children to end this unit. By this point, students had grown fairly comfortable talking about scary things and were more willing to admit to their fears. Using the categories they defined previously on the giant bar graph, they took a poll to see how many in the class were afraid of things in each category. The teacher went through the categories one by one.

▨ **Extension**

Anyone who is afraid of anything in the animal category, stand up.
Anyone who is afraid of anything in the monster category, stand up.

Students were allowed to stand up for more than one category. Each time, a student counted how many were in the category, and the teacher quickly made a graph on the chalkboard. Students were fascinated with how many people were in each category. Their final graph looked like this:

				17	
				X	
				X	
		14		X	
		X		X	
12		X		X	
X		X	11	X	
X		X	X	X	10
X	9	X	X	X	X
X	X	X	X	X	X
X	X	X	X	X	X
X	X	X	X	X	X
X	X	X	X	X	X
X	X	X	X	X	X
X	X	X	X	X	X
X	X	X	X	X	X
Nightmares	Scary Movies	Monsters	Dark Places	Animals	Getting Hurt

Assessment: Looking at Students' Data Representations

What interests second and third graders is the particulars of the data. They are intrigued that Olga's dad was afraid of spiders, or that Ayaz's aunt used to think there was a monster under the bed when she was in second grade. In their representations, seven- and eight-year-old students often want to retain the individuality of each piece of data. They enjoy identifying individual names on their graphs or portraying the characteristics of their data through pictures.

Unlike upper elementary students, second and third graders are not quite ready to pull their attention away from individuals in order to summarize or describe a whole group. This interest in the individual and the particular leads to representations that are some mixture of picture, story, graph, and chart. Some students tend to use words and lists. Others tend to use a pictorial approach.

When encouraged to represent the data in their own way, students at this age can create beautiful and effective representations using color, both for the pictures and to set apart the different categories. Students' picture graphs will not necessarily follow the conventions of graph making that we would expect upper elementary students to use. Their pictures may not be all the same size, or categories may not be lined up so that the number of things in each category can be compared directly. However, when students adopt the conventions of what they think graphs are "supposed" to look like, they often produce mundane bar graphs that actually do not communicate much information.

Encourage students to use their creativity and inventiveness in making their presentation graphs, so that someone who looked at the graph would be as intrigued as they are by the data.

DIALOGUE BOX

Will the Same Categories Work?

The class is looking at a bar graph showing categories of things they find scary. In this discussion during the activity What Scared Adults? (p. 79), students are deciding whether any of the data they collected on things that scare adults could fit in the categories.

Chen: My dad was afraid of dogs, so his could fit in ANIMALS.

Jeffrey: And my aunt's could too. Hers was spiders.

So we definitely have some scary things that fit in the ANIMALS category. Are there any others that you think fit in some of our categories?

Laura: Well, what Temara said about going up to a house on Halloween and the guy jumped out with a pumpkin. That could go in HAUNTED HOUSES.

Tory: And mine can, too, about my mom and the house with the vacant lot.

OK, so there are some other fears that are similar to ours. What else do you notice about things on the adult list? Anything that doesn't fit with our categories?

Simon: Being afraid of getting hit in school.

Olga: Thunderstorms. We didn't have anybody afraid of thunderstorms.

Trini: That could go with DARK, though.

Do you think that thunderstorms could go in our DARK category?

Lila: I don't think so, because what's scary about thunderstorms is the lightning and the thunder, and our dark things were like alleys and basements.

You think our dark things were different? Do other people have opinions?

Ayaz: Yes, they're like places.

So you wouldn't put thunderstorms with DARK? Is there anything else on the adult list that might go with thunderstorms?

Tim: Yes, my mom's friend said he used to be afraid of the ocean.

You think that goes with thunderstorms?

Tim: Yes.

Can you explain how they go together?

Tim: [*pause, shrugs*]

Well, maybe someone else can think of the words for it because I can see how ocean and thunderstorms might go together. Can anyone else add to Tim's idea?

Simon: Maybe because they're both wild and they can push you.

Karina: The ocean can make big crashing sounds like thunder.

Ebony: And you get wet in the ocean and you get wet in a thunderstorm.

Those are interesting ideas. In your groups, you'll have to make some decisions about which things you think go together.

Ping: I have another one that doesn't fit—getting lost. Nobody in the class said getting lost.

Today's Number

Today's Number is one of the routines that are built into the grade 2 *Investigations* curriculum. Routines provide students with regular practice in important mathematical ideas such as number combinations, counting and estimating data, and concepts of time. For Today's Number, which is done daily (or most days), students write equations that equal the number of days they have been in school. Each day, the class generates ways to make that number. For example, on the tenth day of school, students look for ways to combine numbers and operations to make 10.

This routine gives students an opportunity to explore some important ideas in number. By generating ways to make the number of the day, they explore:

■ number composition and part-whole relationships (for example, 10 can be 4 + 6, 5 + 5, or 20 – 10)

■ equivalent arithmetical expressions

■ different operations

■ ways of deriving new numerical expressions by systematically modifying prior ones (for example, 5 + 5 = 10, so 5 + 6 = 11)

Students' strategies evolve over time, becoming more sophisticated as the year progresses. Early in the year, second graders use familiar numbers and combinations, such as 5 + 5 = 10. As they become accustomed to the routine, they begin to see patterns in the combinations and have favorite kinds of number sentences. Later in the year, they draw on their experiences and increased understanding of number. For example, on the forty-ninth day they might include 100 – 51, or even 1000 – 951 in their list of ways to make 49. The types of number sentences that students contribute over time can provide you with a window into their thinking and their levels of understanding of numbers.

If you are doing the full-year grade 2 curriculum, Today's Number is introduced in the first unit, *Mathematical Thinking at Grade 2.*

Throughout the curriculum, variations are often introduced as whole-class activities and then carried on in the Start-Up section. The Start-Up section at the beginning of each session offers suggestions of variations and extensions of Today's Number.

While it is important to do Today's Number every day, it is not necessary to do it during math time. In fact, many teachers have successfully included Today's Number as part of their regular routines at the beginning or end of each day. Other teachers incorporate Today's Number into the odd 10 or 15 minutes that exist before lunch or before a transition time.

If you are teaching an *Investigations* unit for the first time, rather than using the number of days you have been in school as Today's Number, you might choose to use the calendar date. (If today is the sixteenth of the month, 16 is Today's Number.) Or you might choose to begin a counting line that does not correspond to the school day number. Each day, add a number to the strip and use this as Today's Number. Begin with the basic activity and then add variations once students become familiar with this routine.

The basic activity is described below, followed by suggested variations.

Materials

■ Chart paper
■ Student Sheet 1, Weekly Log
■ Interlocking cubes

If you are doing the basic activity, you will also need the following materials:

■ Index cards (cut in half and numbered with the days of school so far, e.g., 1 through 5 for the first week of school)

■ Strips of adding-machine tape

■ Blank 200 chart (tape two blank 100 charts together to form a 10-by-20 grid)

Continued on next page

Basic Activity

Initially, you will want to use Today's Number in a whole group, starting the first week of school. After a short time, students will be familiar with the routine and be ready to use it independently.

Establishing the Routine

Step 1. Post the chart paper. Call students' attention to the small box on their Weekly Log in which they have been recording the number of days they have been in school.

Step 2. Record Today's Number. Write the number of the day at the top of the chart paper. Ask students to suggest ways of making that total.

Step 3. List the number sentences students suggest. Record their suggestions on chart paper. As you do so, invite the group to confirm each suggestion or discuss any incorrect responses, and to explain their thinking. You might have interlocking cubes available for students to double-check number sentences.

Step 4. Introduce the class counting strip. Show students the number cards you made and explain that the class is going to create a counting strip. Each day, the number of the day will be added to the row of cards. Post the cards in order in a visible area.

Step 5. Introduce the 200 chart. Display the blank chart and explain that another way the class will keep track of the days in school is by filling in the chart. Record the appropriate numbers in the chart. Tell the class that each day the number of the day will be added to the chart. To help bring attention to landmark numbers on the chart, ask questions such as, "How many more days until the tenth day of school? the twentieth day?"

Variations

When students are familiar with the structure of Today's Number, you can connect it to the number work they are doing in particular units.

Make Today's Number Ask students to use some of the following to represent the number:

- only addition
- only subtraction
- both addition and subtraction
- three numbers
- combinations of 10 ($23 = 4 + 6 + 4 + 6 + 3$ or $23 = 1 + 9 + 2 + 8 + 3$)
- a double ($36 = 18 + 18$ or $36 = 4 + 4 + 5 + 5 + 9 + 9$)
- multiples of 5 and 10 ($52 = 10 + 10 + 10 + 10 + 10 + 2$ or $52 = 5 + 15 + 20 + 10 + 2$)

Introduce the idea of working backward. Put the number sentences for Today's Number on the board and ask students to determine what number you are expressing: $10 + 3 + 5 + 7 + 5 + 4 = ?$ Notice how students add this string of numbers. Do they use combinations of 10 or doubles to help them?

In addition to defining how Today's Number is expressed, you can vary how and when the activity is done:

Start the Day with Today's Number Post the day's chart paper ahead of time. When students begin arriving, they can generate number sentences and check them with partners, then record their ways to make the number of the day before school begins. Students can review the list of ways to make the number at that time or at the beginning of math class. At whole-group meeting or morning meeting, add the day's number to the 200 chart and the counting strip.

Continued on next page

Choice Time Post chart paper with the Number of the Day written on it so that it is accessible to students. As one of their choices, students generate number sentences and check them with partners, then record them on the chart paper.

Work with a Partner Each student works with a partner for 5 to 10 minutes and lists some ways to make the day's number. Partners check each other's work. Pairs bring their lists to the class meeting or sharing time. Students have their lists of number sentences in their math folders. These can be used as a record of students' growth in working with number over the school year.

Homework Assign Today's Number as homework. Students share number sentences sometime during class the following day.

Catch-Up It can be easy to get a few days behind in this routine, so here are two ways to catch up. Post two or three Number-of-the-Day pages for students to visit during Choice Time or free time. Or assign a Number of the Day to individual students. Each can generate number sentences for his or her number as well as collect number sentences from classmates.

Class History Post "special messages" below the day's number card to create a timeline about your class. Special messages can include birthdays, teeth lost, field trips, memorable events, as well as math riddles.

Today's Number Book Collect the Today's Number charts in a *Number-of-the-Day Book*. Arrange the pages in order, creating chapters based on 10's. Chapter 1, for example, is ways to make the numbers 1 through 10, and combinations for numbers 11–20 become Chapter 2.

How Many Pockets?

How Many Pockets? is one of the classroom routines presented in the grade 2 *Investigations* curriculum. Routines provide students with regular practice in important mathematical ideas such as number combinations, counting and estimating data, and concepts of time. In How Many Pockets? students collect, represent, and interpret numerical data about the number of pockets everyone in the class is wearing on a particular day. This routine often becomes known as Pocket Day. In addition to providing opportunities for comparison of data, Pocket Days provide a meaningful context in which students work purposefully with counting and grouping. Pocket Day experiences contribute to the development of students' number sense—the ability to use numbers flexibly and to see relationships among numbers.

If you are doing the full-year grade 2 *Investigations* curriculum, collect pocket data at regular intervals throughout the year. Many teachers collect pocket data every tenth day of school.

The basic activity is described below, followed by suggested variations. Variations are introduced within the context of the *Investigations* units. If you are not doing the full grade 2 curriculum, begin with the basic activity and then add variations when students become familiar with this routine.

Materials

- Interlocking cubes
- Large jar
- Large rubber band or tape
- Hundred Number Wall Chart and number cards (1–100)
- Pocket Data Chart (teacher made)
- Class list of names
- Chart paper

1	2	3	4	5	6	7	8	9	10
11	12	13	14	15	16	17	18	19	20
21	22	23	24	25	26	27	28	29	30
31	32	33	34	35	36	37	38	39	40
41	42	43	44	45	46	47	48	49	50
51	52	53	54	55	56	57	58	59	60
61	62	63	64	65	66	67	68	69	70
71	72	73	74	75	76	77	78	79	80
81	82	83	84	85	86	87	88	89	90
91	92	93	94	95	96	97	98	99	100

Hundred Number Wall Chart

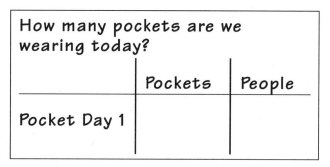

How many pockets are we wearing today?

	Pockets	People
Pocket Day 1		

Pocket Data Chart

Basic Activity

Step 1. Students estimate how many pockets the class is wearing today. Students share their estimates and their reasoning. Record the estimates on chart paper. As the Pocket Days continue through the year, students' estimates may be based on the data recorded on past Pocket Days.

Continued on next page

Step 2. Students count their pockets. Each student takes one interlocking cube for each pocket he or she is wearing.

Step 3. Students put the cubes representing their pockets in a large jar. Vary the way you do this. For example, rather than passing the jar around the group, call on students with specific numbers of pockets to put their cubes in the jar (for example, students with 3 pockets). Use numeric criteria to determine who puts cubes in the jar (for example, students with more than 5 but fewer than 8 pockets). Mark the level of cubes on the jar with a rubber band or tape.

Step 4. With students, agree on a way to count the cubes. Count the cubes to find the total number of pockets. Ask students for ideas about how to double-check the count. By recounting in another way, students see that a group of objects can be counted in more than one way, for example, by 1's, 2's, 5's, and 10's. With many experiences, they begin to realize that some ways of counting are more efficient than others, and that a group of items can be counted in ways other than by 1 without changing the total.

Primary students are usually most secure counting by 1's, and that is often their method of choice. Experiences with counting and grouping in other ways help them begin to see that number is conserved or remains the same regardless of its arrangement—20 cubes is 20 whether counted by 1's, 2's, or 5's. Students also become more flexible in their ability to use grouping, especially important in our number system, in which grouping by 10 is key.

Step 5. Record the total for the day on a Pocket Data Chart. Maintaining a chart of the pocket data as they are accumulated provides natural opportunities for students to see that data can change over time and to compare quantities.

How many pockets are we wearing today?	Pockets	People
Pocket Day 1	41	29

Variations

Comparing Data Students revisit the data from the previous Pocket Day and the corresponding cube level marked on the now empty jar.

On the last Pocket Day, we counted [*give number*] pockets. Do you think we will be wearing more, fewer, or about the same number of pockets today? Why?

After students explain their reasoning, continue with the basic activity. When the cubes have been collected, invite students to compare the present level of cubes with the previous level indicated by the tape or rubber bands and to revise their estimates based on this visual information.

Discuss the revised estimates and then complete the activity. After you add the day's total to the Pocket Data Chart, ask students to compare and interpret the data. To facilitate discussion, build a train of interlocking cubes for today's and the previous Pocket Day's number. As students compare the trains, elicit what the cube trains represent and why they have different numbers of cubes.

Use the Hundred Number Wall Chart Do the basic activity, but this time let students choose only one way to count the cubes. Then introduce the Hundred Number Wall Chart as a tool that can be used for counting cubes. This is easiest when done with students sitting on the floor in a circle.

Continued on next page

To check our pocket count, we'll put our cubes in the pockets on the chart. A pocket can have just one cube, so we'll put one cube in number 1's pocket, the next cube in number 2's pocket, and keep going in the same way. How many cubes can we put in the first row?

Students will probably see that 10 cubes will fill the first row of the chart.

One group of 10 cubes fits in this row. What if we complete the second row? How many rows of the chart do you think we will fill with the cubes we counted today?

Encourage students to share their thinking. Then have them count with you and help to place the cubes one by one in the pockets on the chart. When finished, examine the chart together, pointing out the total number of cubes in it and the number of complete rows. For each row, snap together the cubes to make a train of 10. As you do so, use the rows to encourage students to consider combining groups of 10. Record the day's total on your Pocket Data Chart.

Note: If cubes do not fit in the pockets of the chart, place the chart on the floor and place the cubes on top of the numbers.

Find the Most Common Number of Pockets
Each student connects the cubes representing his or her pockets into a train. Before finding the total number of pockets, sort the cube trains with students to find the most common number of pockets. Pose and investigate additional questions, such as:

- **How many people are wearing the greatest number of pockets?**
- **Is there a number of pockets no one is wearing?**
- **Who has the fewest pockets?**

The cubes are then counted to determine the total number of pockets.

Take a Closer Look at Pocket Data Each student builds a cube train representing his or her pockets. Beginning with those who have zero

pockets, call on students to bring their cube trains to the front of the room. Record the information in a chart, such as the one shown here. You might make a permanent chart with blanks for placing number cards.

_0_ people have 0 pockets.	_0 pockets_
_4_ people have 1 pocket.	_4 pockets_
_2_ people have 2 pockets.	_4 pockets_
_2_ people have 3 pockets.	_6 pockets_

Pose questions about the data, such as, "Two people have 2 pockets. How many pockets is that?" Then record the number of pockets.

To work with combining groups, you might keep a running total of pockets as data are recorded in the chart until you have found the cumulative total.

We counted [12] pockets, and then we counted [6] pockets. How many pockets have we counted so far? Be ready to tell us how you thought about it.

As students give their solutions, encourage them to share their mental strategies. Alternatively, after all data have been collected, students can work on the problem of finding the total number of pockets.

Graph Pocket Data Complete the activity using the variation Find the Most Common Number of Pockets. Leave students' cube trains intact. Each student then creates a representation of the day's pocket data. Provide a variety of materials, including stick-on notes, stickers or paper squares, markers and crayons, drawing paper, and graph paper for students to use.

Continued on next page

These cube trains represent how many pockets people are wearing today. Suppose you want to show our pocket data to your family, friends, or students in another classroom. How could you show our pocket data on paper so that someone else could see what we found out about our pockets today?

By creating their own representations, students become more familiar with the data and may begin to develop theories as they consider how to communicate what they know about the data to an audience. Students' representations may not be precise; what's important is that the representations enable them to describe and interpret their data.

Compare Pocket Data with Another Class
Arrange ahead of time to compare pocket data with a fourth- or fifth-grade class. Present the following question to students:

Do you think fifth-grade students wear more, fewer, or about the same number of pockets as second-grade students? Why?

Discuss students' thinking. Then investigate this question by comparing your data with data from another classroom. One way to do this is to invite the other class to participate in your Pocket Day. Do the activity first with the second graders, recording how many people have each number of pockets on the Pocket Data Chart and finding the total number of pockets. Repeat with the other students, recording their data on chart paper. Then compare the two sets of data.

How does the number of pockets in the fifth grade compare to the number of pockets in second grade?

Discuss students' ideas.

Calculate the Total Number of Pockets Divide students into groups of four or five. Each group determines the total number of pockets being worn by the group. Data from each small group are shared and recorded on the board. Using this information, students work in pairs to determine the total number of pockets worn by the class. As a group, they share strategies used for determining the total number of pockets.

In another variation, students share individual pocket data with the group. Each student records this information using a class list of names to keep track. They then determine the total number of pockets worn by the students in the class. Observe how students calculate the total number of pockets. What materials do they use? Do they group familiar numbers together, such as combinations of 10, doubles, or multiples of 5?

Time and Time Again

Time and Time Again is one of the classroom routines included in the grade 2 *Investigations* curriculum. This routine helps students develop an understanding of time-related ideas such as sequencing of events, the passage of time, duration of time periods, and identifying important times in their day.

Because many of the ideas and suggestions presented in this routine will be incorporated throughout the school day and into other parts of the curriculum, we encourage teachers to use this routine in whatever way meets the needs of their students and their classroom. We believe that learning about time and understanding ideas about time happen best when activities are presented *over* time and have relevance to students' experiences and lives.

Daily Schedule Post a daily schedule. Identify important times (start of school, math, music, recess, reading) using both analog (clockface) and digital (10:15) representations. Discuss the daily schedule each day and encourage students to compare the actual starting time of, say, math class with what is posted on the schedule.

Talk Time Identify times as you talk with students. For example, "In 15 minutes we will be cleaning up and going to recess." Include specific times and refer to a clock in your classroom, "It is now 10:15. In 15 minutes we will be cleaning up and going out to recess. That will be at 10:30."

Timing One Hour Set a timer to go off at 1-hour intervals. Choose a starting time and write both the analog time (use a clockface) and the digital time. When the timer rings, record the time using analog and digital times. At the end of the day, students make observations about the data collected. Initially you'll want to use whole and half hours as your starting points. Gradually you can use times that are 10 or 20 minutes after the hour and also appoint students to be in charge of the timer and of recording the times.

Timing Other Intervals Set a timer to go off at 15-minute intervals over a period of 2 hours. Begin at the hour and, after the data have been collected, discuss with students what happened each time 15 minutes was added to the time (11:00, 11:15, 11:30, 11:45). You can also try this with 10-minute intervals.

Home Schedule Students make a schedule of important times at home. They can do this both for school days and for nonschool days. They should include both analog and digital times on their schedules. Later in the year they can use this schedule to see if they were really on time for things like dinner, piano lessons, or bedtime. They record the actual time that events happened and calculate how early or late they were. Students can illustrate their schedules.

Comparing Schedules Partners compare important times in their day, such as what time they eat dinner, go to bed, get up, leave for school. They can compare whether events are earlier or later, and some students might want to calculate how much earlier or later these events occur.

Life Timelines Students create a timeline of their lives. They interview family members and collect information about important developmental milestones such as learning to walk, first word, first day of school, first lost tooth, and important family events. Students then record these events on a timeline that is a representation of the first 7 or 8 years of their lives.

Clock Data Students collect data about the types of clocks they have in their home—digital or analog. They make a representation of these data and as a class compare their results.

- **Are there more digital or analog clocks in your house?**
- **Is this true of our class set of data?**
- **How could we compare our individual data to a class set of data?**

Continued on next page

Time Collection   Students bring in things from home that have to do with time. Include digital and analog clocks as well as timers of various sorts. These items could be sorted and grouped in different ways. Some students may be interested in investigating different types of time-pieces such as sundials, sand timers, and pendulums.

How Long Is a Minute?   As you time 1 minute, students close their eyes and then raise their hands when they think a minute has gone by. Ask, "Is a minute longer or shorter than you imagined?" Repeat this activity or have students do this with partners. You can also do this activity with a half-minute.

What Can You Do in a Minute?   When students are familiar with timing 1 minute, they work in pairs and collect data about things they can do in 1 minute. Brainstorm a list of events that students might try. Some ideas that second graders have suggested include: writing their names; doing jumping jacks or sit-ups; hopping on one foot; saying the ABC's; snapping together inter-locking cubes; writing certain numbers or letters (this is great practice for working on reversals); and drawing geometric shapes such as triangles, squares, or stars. Each student chooses four or five activities to do in 1 minute. Before they collect the data, they predict how many they can do in 1 minute. Then with partners they gather the data and compare.

How Long Does It Take?   Using a stopwatch or a clock with a second hand, time how long it takes students to complete certain tasks such as lining up, giving out supplies, or cleaning up after math time. Emphasize doing these things in a responsible way. Students can take turns being "timekeepers."

Stopwatches   Most second graders are fascinated by stopwatches. You will find that students come up with many ideas about what to time. If possible, acquire one for your classroom. (Inexpensive ones are available through educational supply catalogs.) Having stopwatches available in the classroom allows students to teach each other about time and how to keep track of time.

The following activities will help ensure that this unit is comprehensible to students who are acquiring English as a second language. The suggested approach is based on *The Natural Approach: Language Acquisition in the Classroom* by Stephen D. Krashen and Tracy D. Terrell (Alemany Press, 1983.) The intent is for second-language learners to acquire new vocabulary in an active, meaningful context.

Note that *acquiring* a word is different from *learning* a word. Depending on their level of proficiency, students may be able to comprehend a word upon hearing it during an investigation, without being able to say it. Other students may be able to use the word orally, but not read or write it. The goal is to help students naturally acquire targeted vocabulary at their present level of proficiency.

We suggest using these activities just before the related investigations. The activities can be led by English-proficient students.

Investigation 3

flies, walks, crawls, swims, hops

1. Cut a picture of a bird from a magazine or locate one in a book. Show the picture to students and explain that birds can fly. Model flying motions through pantomime.

2. Repeat this activity for animals that walk (for example, cat, dog), swim (for example, fish, duck), crawl (for example, worm, snake), and hop (for example, rabbit, grasshopper, frog).

Blackline Masters

_____ , 19 ____

Dear Family,

Our class is beginning a new mathematics unit called *Does It Walk, Crawl, or Swim?* In this unit, your child will collect data (information about people or groups of objects) and will learn about sorting and classifying the data. Once data are collected, they have to be organized in some way so that they can be analyzed and compared. Children begin the unit by playing Guess My Rule—a game in which they analyze data and try to figure what is alike.

Children continue the unit with data collection projects. They collect data about objects that sink and float, about what animals can be found in the neighborhood, and in what ways these animals move about. Children will invent ways of organizing and presenting the data they collect and also use some traditional ways such as making graphs and drawing pictures.

You can become involved in this unit as your child may ask you what it was that scared you when you were his or her age. Help your child record your answers, since they will be the basis for work in class.

You can help your child in other ways.

- For homework your child will be playing Guess My Rule with about 20 household objects. Your child will teach you and other family members this game. Guess My Rule is also fun to play in a large group of people (family party, after-school club).

- Your child might be interested in working with the sink-and-float experiment at home. Ask your child to explain this experiment to you and, if possible, together investigate other objects that sink and float.

- Your child will also be collecting some information from you that will become part of a set of data that we will be using in the classroom. You might need to help your child write this information.

- Finally, as you are reading the newspaper or watching the news, point out graphs and charts to your child. We live in an information-rich society, and it is important for students to begin to experience the variety of ways that information is communicated and represented in the world.

We hope you will enjoy working with your child to become more familiar with ways we collect and organize data.

Sincerely,

Weekly Log

Day Box

Monday, _____

Tuesday, _____

Wednesday, _____

Thursday, _____

Friday, _____

© Dale Seymour Publications®

Guess My Rule Questions

There are 28 students in a class. The class played Guess My Rule using the rule "wearing shoes with laces." There were 12 children wearing shoes with laces. How many children were not wearing shoes with laces?

Show your thinking using pictures, numbers, or words.

On the back, make a representation of the class's data for the rule "wearing shoes with laces."

Today's Number

Make Today's Number, _____, in at least 5 ways. You may ask someone else in your family to think of another way and record it here as well.

101

Name _____ Date _____

Yektti Stories

Write a story about the Yekttis. Include information about what they eat, what they do for work and for fun, if they live in families, and what their home planet is like. You may include a picture showing a whole Yektti. Use more paper if you need to.

© Dale Seymour Publications®

Investigation 1 • Resource
Does It Walk, Crawl, or Swim?

© Dale Seymour Publications®

Investigation 1 • Resource
Does It Walk, Crawl, or Swim?

© Dale Seymour Publications®

Investigation 1 • Resource
Does It Walk, Crawl, or Swim?

© Dale Seymour Publications®

Investigation 1 • Resource
Does It Walk, Crawl, or Swim?

© Dale Seymour Publications®

© Dale Seymour Publications®

Investigation 1 • Resource
Does It Walk, Crawl, or Swim?

© Dale Seymour Publications®

Investigation 1 • Resource
Does It Walk, Crawl, or Swim?

© Dale Seymour Publications®

Investigation 1 • Resource
Does It Walk, Crawl, or Swim?

© Dale Seymour Publications®

© Dale Seymour Publications®

Investigation 1 • Resource
Does It Walk, Crawl, or Swim?

© Dale Seymour Publications®

Investigation 1 • Resource
Does It Walk, Crawl, or Swim?

© Dale Seymour Publications®

Investigation 1 • Resource
Does It Walk, Crawl, or Swim?

© Dale Seymour Publications®

© Dale Seymour Publications®

Investigation 1 • Resource
Does It Walk, Crawl, or Swim?

© Dale Seymour Publications®

© Dale Seymour Publications®

Investigation 1 • Resource
Does It Walk, Crawl, or Swim?

© Dale Seymour Publications®

Investigation 1 • Resource
Does It Walk, Crawl, or Swim?

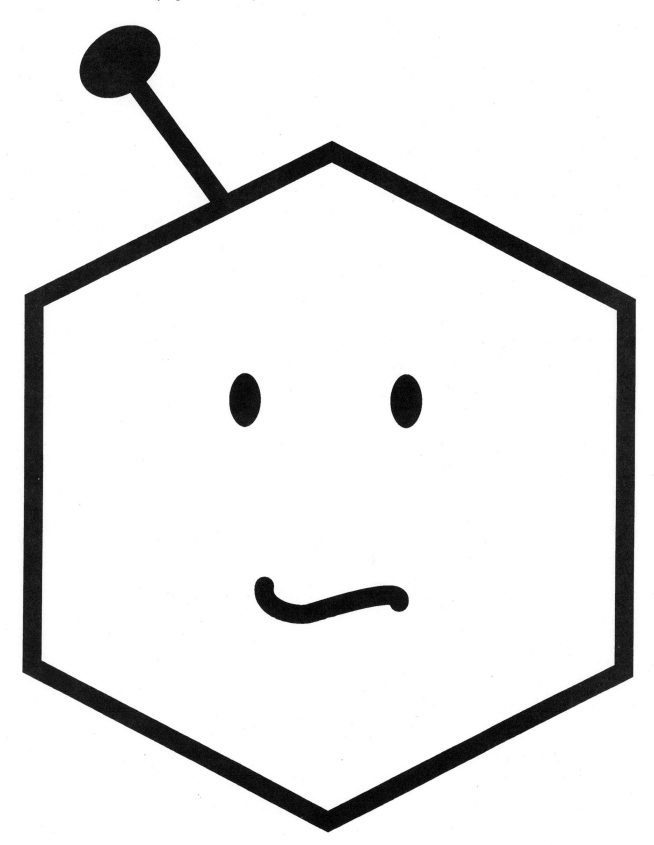

© Dale Seymour Publications®

Investigation 1 • Resource
Does It Walk, Crawl, or Swim?

© Dale Seymour Publications®

Investigation 1 • Resource
Does It Walk, Crawl, or Swim?

© Dale Seymour Publications®

© Dale Seymour Publications®

Investigation 1 • Resource
Does It Walk, Crawl, or Swim?

© Dale Seymour Publications®

Investigation 1 • Resource
Does It Walk, Crawl, or Swim?

134

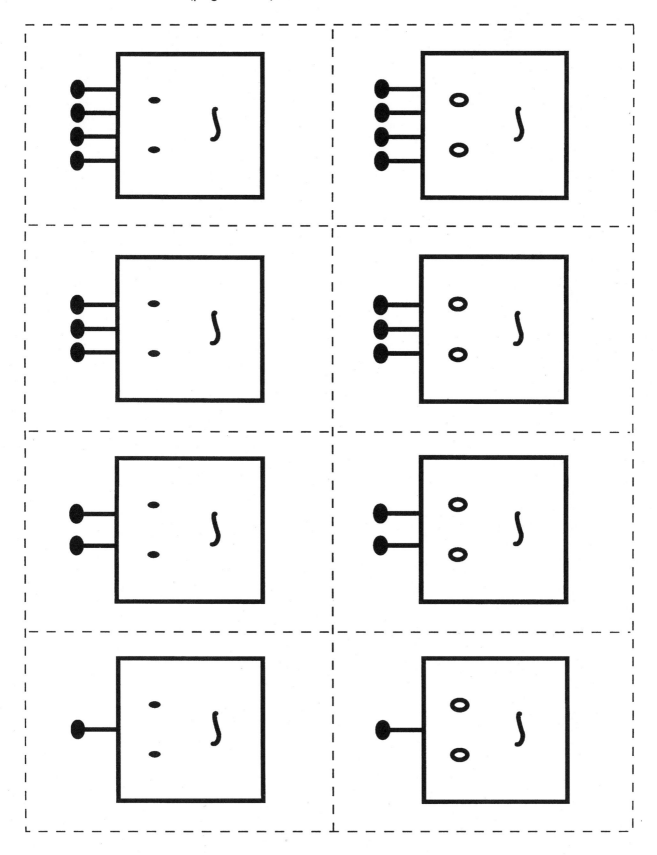

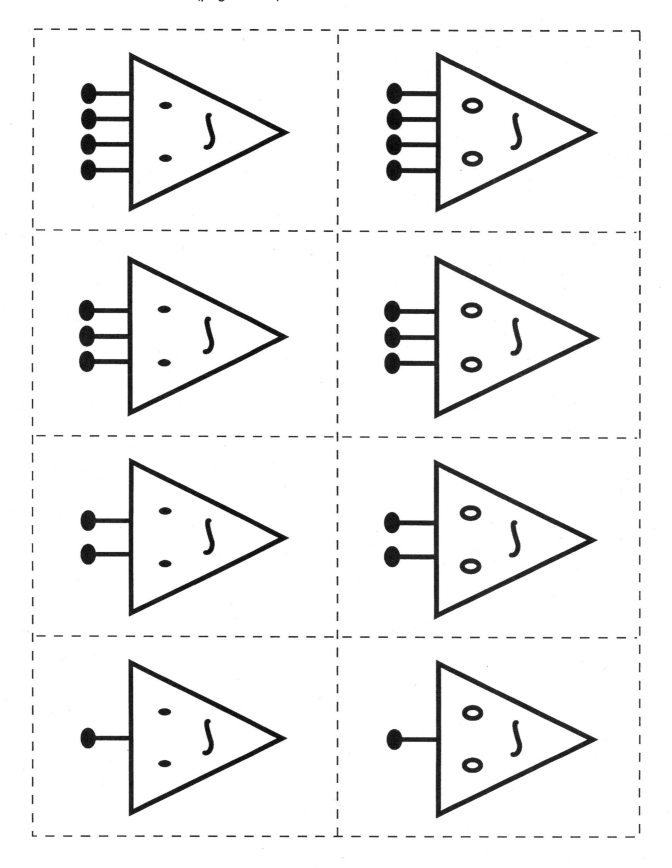

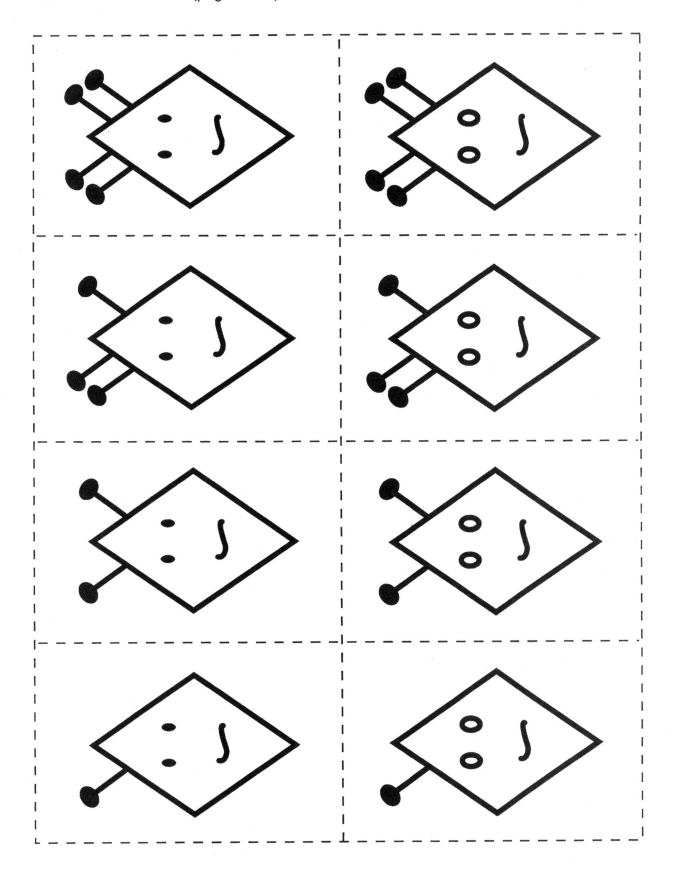

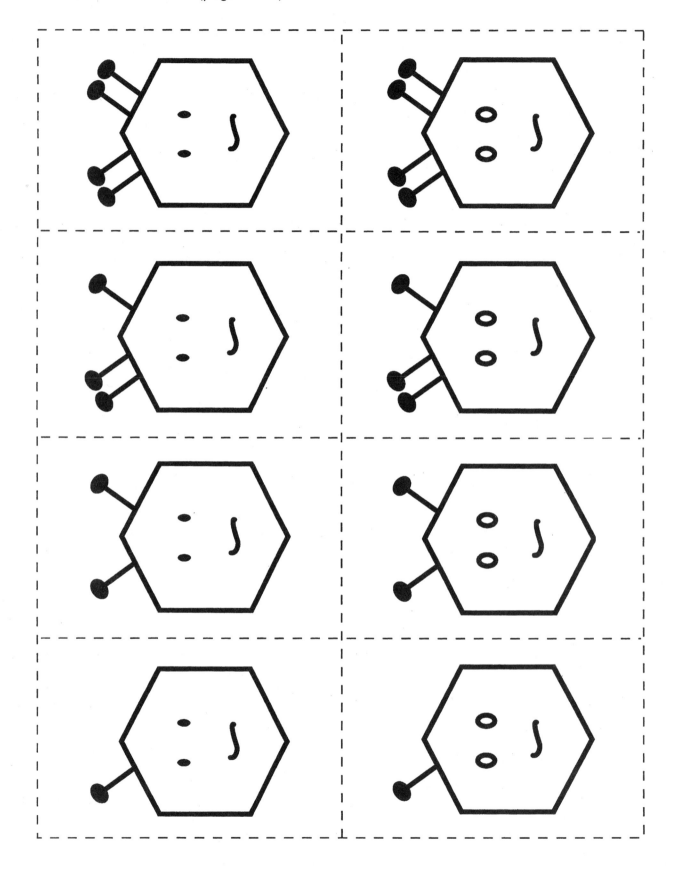

square	hexagon
triangle	diamond
plain eyes	ringed eyes
1 antenna	2 antennae
3 antennae	4 antennae

© Dale Seymour Publications®

Guess My Rule with Thing Collections

Materials: a Thing Collection made of 15–20 small objects that are all different from each other, such as a spoon, a penny, a crayon, a paper clip, a safety pin, a small block, a birthday candle, and so on.

How to Play

The object of the game is to figure out the Mystery Rule by trying to place objects from the Thing Collection into one of two categories.

1. The rule maker decides on a Mystery Rule for sorting the Thing Collection into two groups: one group that fits the rule and one group that doesn't fit the rule. For example, a rule might be "made of plastic" or "is red."

2. The rule maker starts the game by showing three objects that fit the rule and two objects that do not fit the rule.

3. The guessers try to find other objects that fit the rule.

4. With each guess, the object is placed in one of two piles: "fits the rule" or "does not fit the rule." Both piles should be clearly visible. The rule maker says if the placement is correct. If it is not, the object is placed in the correct group.

5. Guessers continue to place objects in the two piles. Once all the objects have been correctly sorted, the guessers guess the rule.

Use the back of this sheet to list the things in Your Thing Collection.

Playing Guess My Rule with Thing Collections

Use your Thing Collection to play Guess My Rule with someone at home. Write one of your mystery rules and make a representation that shows how the collection was sorted for that rule.

Mystery Rule _____

On the back, write another rule and make a representation of how you sorted your collection using that rule.

ONE-CIRCLE DIAGRAM

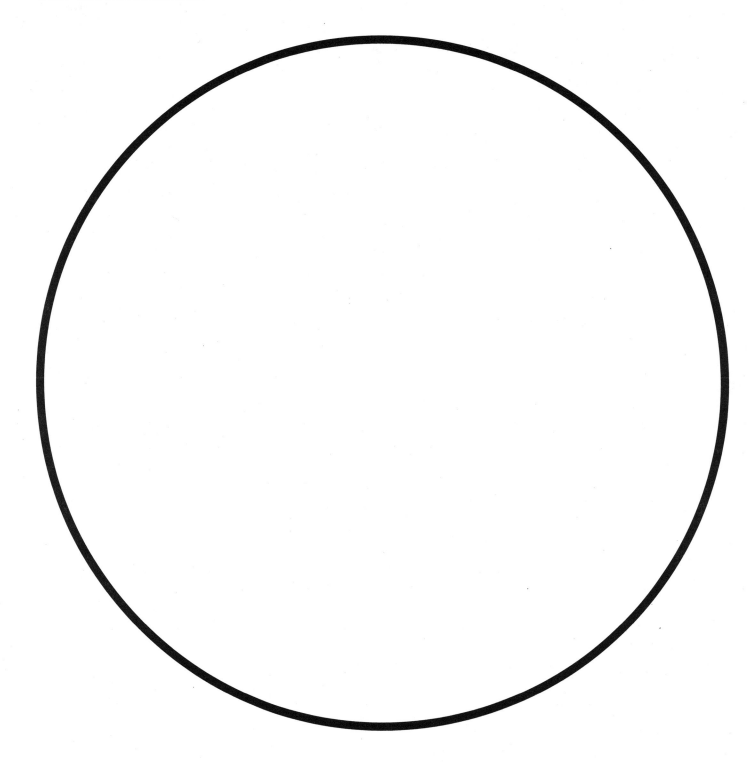

© Dale Seymour Publications®

142

Animals in the Neighborhood

1. What question did you answer about the animals in your neighborhood?

_____

2. What categories did you use to sort your data?

_____

3. Draw a picture of the representation you made of your data.

_____

4. What are three interesting things you noticed about your data? Write them on the back of this paper.

Animals Near My Home

Look carefully in, around, and near your home for any kind of animal. The animal may be the tiniest bug or a large, furry creature! Draw or write about your findings.

What category or categories might this animal fit? If you see more than one animal, what different categories might they fit? You may use the back of this sheet.

Adult Scary Things Data

Our survey question for adults:

_____

_____

_____

Answers from the adults I asked:

1. _____

_____

2. _____

_____

3. _____

_____

4. _____

_____

Solving Problems with Imaginary Data

This imaginary class talked about what students were afraid of most. Here are the data they collected:

scary movies   5   getting hurt   6

dark places   4   monsters   3

animals   7

How many students are in this imaginary class?
How do you know? Show your thinking in pictures, numbers, or words.

The same imaginary class then collected data about the question: "Are you afraid of scary dreams?" Twelve children said "yes." How many children said "no?" How do you know? Show your thinking on the back of this sheet.

Practice Pages

This optional section provides homework ideas for teachers who want or need to give more homework than is assigned to accompany the activities in this unit. The problems included here provide additional practice in learning about number relationships and in solving computation and number problems. For number units, you may want to use some of these if your students need more work in these areas or if you want to assign daily homework. For other units, you can use these problems so that students can continue to work on developing number and computation sense while they are focusing on other mathematical content in class. We recommend that you introduce activities in class before assigning related problems for homework.

Tens Go Fish   Students play this game in the units *Mathematical Thinking at Grade 2* and *Coins, Coupons, and Combinations.* If your students are familiar with the game, you can simply send home the directions and Number Cards so that students can play at home. If your students have not played the game before, introduce it in class and have students play once or twice before sending it home. You might have students do this activity two times for homework in this unit.

Turn Over 10   Students play this game in the units *Mathematical Thinking at Grade 2* and *Coins, Coupons, and Combinations.* If your students are familiar with the game, you can simply send home the directions and Number Cards so that students can play at home. If your students have not played the game before, introduce it in class and have students play once or twice before sending it home. You might have students do this activity two times for homework in this unit.

Story Problems   Story problems at various levels of difficulty are used throughout the *Investigations* curriculum. The two story problem sheets provided here help students review and maintain skills that have already been taught. You can make up other problems in this format, using numbers and contexts that are appropriate for your students. Students solve the problems and then record their strategies, using numbers, words, and pictures.

People and Pet Riddles   This type of problem is introduced in the unit *Coins, Coupons, and Combinations.* Here, one problem sheet is provided. You can also make up other problems in this format, using numbers that are appropriate for your students. For this problem sheet, students solve the problem and then record their strategies, using numbers, words, or pictures.

Tens Go Fish

Materials: Deck of Number Cards 0–10 (four of each) with the wild cards removed

Players: 3 to 4

How to Play

The object of the game is to get two cards that total 10.

1. Each player is dealt five cards. The rest of the cards are placed face down in the center of the table.

2. If you have any pairs of cards that total 10, put them down in front of you and replace those cards with cards from the deck.

3. Take turns. On a turn, ask <u>one</u> other player for a card that will go with a card in your hand to make 10.

4. If you get a card that makes 10, put the pair of cards down. Take one card from the deck. Your turn is over.

   If you do not get a card that makes 10, take the top card from the deck. Your turn is over.

   If the card you take from the deck makes 10 with a card in your hand, put the pair down and take another card.

5. If there are no cards left in your hand but still cards in the deck, you take two cards.

6. The game is over when there are no more cards.

7. At the end of the game, make a list of the number pairs you made.

Turn Over 10

Materials: Deck of Number Cards 0–10 (four of each) plus four wild cards

Players: 2 to 3

How to Play

The object of the game is to turn over and collect combinations of cards that total 10.

1. Arrange the cards face down in four rows of five cards. Place the rest of the deck face down in a pile.

2. Take turns. On a turn, turn over one card and then another. A wild card can be made into any number.

    If the total is less than 10, turn over another card.

    If the total is more than 10, your turn is over and the cards are turned face down in the same place.

    If the total is 10, take the cards and replace them with cards from the deck. You get another turn.

3. Place each of your card combinations of 10 in separate piles so they don't get mixed up.

4. The game is over when no more 10's can be made.

5. At the end of the game, make a list of the number combinations for 10 that you made.

0	0	0	0
1	1	1	1
2	2	2	2

3	3	3	3
4	4	4	4
5	5	5	5

Practice Page
Does It Walk, Crawl, or Swim?

6	6	6	6
7	7	7	7
8	8	8	8

Practice Page
Does It Walk, Crawl, or Swim?

9	9	9	9
10	10	10	10
Wild Card	Wild Card	Wild Card	Wild Card

© Dale Seymour Publications®

Practice Page
Does It Walk, Crawl, or Swim?

Practice Page A

I have 26 pennies. My sister has 15 pennies. How many do we have in all?

Show how you solved this problem. You can use numbers, words, or pictures.

Practice Page B

Rachel has 38 crayons in a box. Her brother borrows 11 crayons. How many does she have left?

Show how you solved this problem. You can use numbers, words, or pictures.

Practice Page C

There are 14 legs in this group.
There are 4 heads in this group.
There are 8 ears in this group.
There are 10 fingers in this group.
There are 3 tails in this group.

Who could be in this group?

Show how you solved this problem. You can use numbers, words, or pictures.